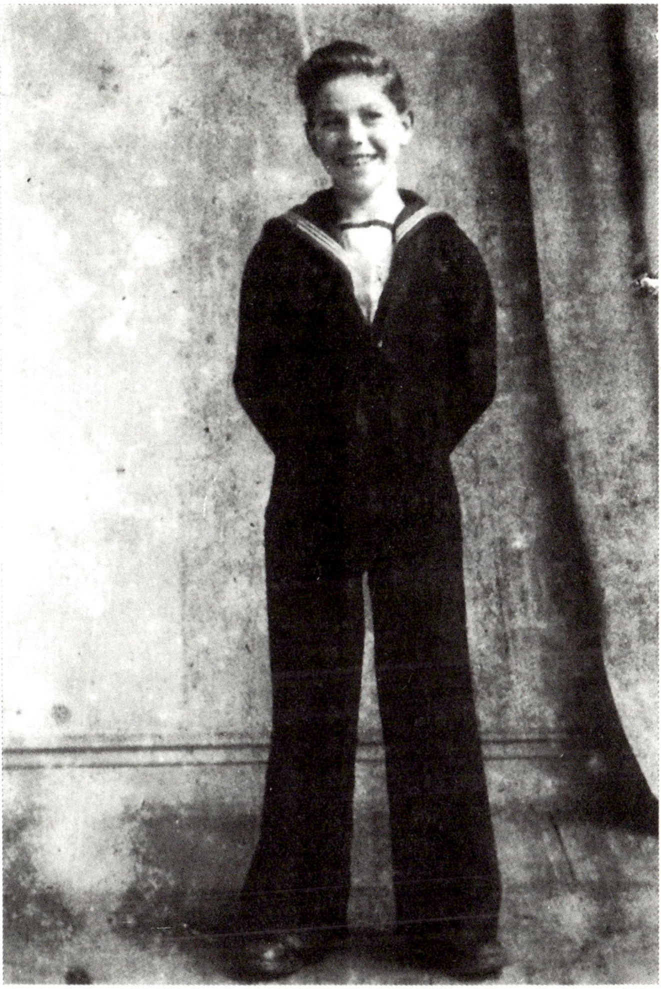

The author aged 15

CLASSIC
MARINE PUBLICATIONS

To
Rosemary and Brian Weedon
from
John Richardson 2006

A Deck Boy's Diary

John Richardson

Classic Marine Publications

First published in 2000 by
Classic Marine Publications
121 Vivian Road
Sketty
Swansea
Glamorgan SA2 0UP

ISBN: 0 9537242 0 4

A Deck Boy's Diary

John Richardson

Printed & Bound by
Lazarus Press
Unit 7 Caddsdown Business Park
Bideford
Devon EX39 3DX

Dedicated to my wife Barbara
and my sons Darren and Colin

CONTENTS

Preface

If somebody had climbed onto a soap box in the year 1950 and proclaimed to the world that within thirty years the British Merchant Navy would be decimated, he wouldn't have had much of an audience. Just a few years after the end of World War Two, shipbuilding in Britain was going on at a fantastic rate with the order books full at all the shipyards. Britain relied heavily on its shipbuilding and merchant service, these two industries alone employed hundreds of thousands of men and women; any mention of the end of the Merchant Navy would have been laughable. However, a little white cloud was beginning to form on the distant horizon. Even in those times, there were a few far-sighted people who could already see the day of the supertankers, the bulk carriers, the roll-on roll-offs and the container ships. They didn't know exactly when, nevertheless they knew they were coming. They could see the little white cloud on the horizon because they'd put it there, and as time went by, those far sighted people would slowly draw that cloud closer and paint it a little darker.

All too often in this day and age we hear of the great Merchant Navy we once had, and the way it had slowly been allowed to fade away into oblivion. The blame for the gradual end of this once great service has always been laid firmly at the feet of successive governments and greedy ship owners. There are also those who to some extent blame the National Union of Seamen, saying that, having been in the pocket of the ship owners for so long, they never did enough at the appropriate time. Although these three groups may have played a significant part in the running of the service, they are only the tip of an iceberg. The real truth about the downfall of the Merchant Navy as we once knew it, was in modernisation, sophisticated business planning, and new technology.

The ship owner has to make money, both for himself and his shareholders – he is a businessman and if he can pay a lower rate of pay, he doesn't really care who mans his ships, and why should he? Sentiment and business don't go well together and anybody who tries to mix the two will often fail. Governments are not concerned who mans the ships either, and why should they? When World War Two ended the men of the Merchant Navy had served their purpose, they were surplus to requirements and weren't needed any more.

Some British shipping companies employed large numbers of foreign seamen; they were bound to do so by the governments of the countries to which they traded and the ship owners were quite happy in doing so. This was not only because it involved lower rates of pay, but also because they were less likely to go on strike. There are no records of course – and neither is there any proof – but after the strikes of the 1950s and 1960s it must have been tempting for ship owners to rid themselves of the British seaman forever.

When I made my first trip to sea in 1953, I remember one of the sailors telling me there were 4,000 ships under the red ensign, each of which were over 5,000 tons gross. I don't know whether these figures were correct and never bothered to find out, however I clearly remember to whatever port we went the red duster was always there, and as soon as one British ship left another would be waiting for its berth. In those times possibly half the British deep sea cargo ships were ten knot tramps, a large number were Empire, Fort, and Liberty ships and each of these could carry a cargo of 10,000 tons. The foreign going oil tankers of the day were not much bigger, each carrying on average 12,000 tons.

By 1950 the big change had aleady begun – even before I made my first trip to sea – when the *Velutina* was launched on the Tyne. She was a monster, and could carry 36,000 tons of oil, but more importantly there was no increase in her number of crew. Even though her operating costs were higher, the *Velutina* could do the work of three current sized tankers and the result was two full crews of a 12,000 tonner could now be dispensed with. The *Velutina* had a number of sister ships – with even bigger ones planned – and for the British merchant seaman it was the beginning of the end.

The 1950s also saw many ship owners change to flags of convenience. The registration charges and taxes, imposed by successive British governments, were so high it forced many British ship owners to change flags, or go bust. Under these flags of convenience the ship owner had more freedom from legislation, paid much lower taxes and registration charges, and could employ cheap uncertificated foreign labour. This often resulted in the ships operating in an unsafe condition. Since the 1950s whenever a marine accident has occurred, invariably the vessel involved has been under the Liberian or Panamanian flag.

During the 1960s, after much planning and deliberation, the container ships and their new terminals came into being. Things were now moving more rapidly than ever before in the history of the mercantile marine, the writing was clearly on the wall and by the 1970s things were in full swing. The little fluffy white cloud which had been on the horizon had now turned into a dark grey nimbus and the end was in sight.

The *City Of Durban*, a 54,000 ton container ship owned jointly by Ellermans and T&J Harrisons, was completed in 1974. She could carry six times as much cargo as the Empire, Fort or Liberty ships, was able to travel at twice their speed, and for faster turnarounds had far superior cargo handling facilities. On top of all that, the *City Of Durban* carried a full crew of no more than thirty-three.

Therefore, combining speed, size and capabilities; on a round trip from the UK to South Africa, it would take roughly twelve of the Empire, Fort or Liberty ships each with a crew of thirty-nine, to compete with a ship like the *City Of Durban*. The result was the disappearance of well over 400 seafarers' jobs in this example alone.

Today we have the bulk carriers which take huge deliveries of iron ore, coal and grain around the world. There are the supertankers, many of which are 350,000 deadweight tons (some even bigger!) and together with their cheap foreign labour crews each one of these giant oil cans can do the work of a 12,000 ton tanker of the 1950s thirty times over. The nett result of one supertanker is a loss of approximately 1,500 seafarers' jobs.

The Merchant Navy hasn't disappeared at all, it is still with us as never before but unfortunately for those who look back over their shoulders, the service is now under the control of huge conglomerates, sailing under flags of convenience and running on cheap foreign labour crews.

§

If you ask any seaman about the ships he's been on and which was the one which had the most impact on him or the one he remembers best, the chances are he'll say it was his first ship. This may not have been the best ship he'd ever been on, and possibly might not even have been a good one, but for some reason many a seaman remembers his first ship better than any other. Even years after completing his first trip to sea and with some fondness, a seaman will still be able to describe his first ship and his shipmates in some detail. On the other hand, if you ask the same person about some of the other vessels in which he'd later served, he probably wouldn't even remember who his cabin mate was, the captain's name, or much else about the vessel.

Everybody in life has a tale to tell, and the idea of my writing this story came about when I was in a sea school in 1951. It was there where I read an account of a boy making his first trip to sea towards the end of the 19th century. He'd kept a rough diary of the daily events on board his first ship, a sailing ship, then at a much later date had his diaries published describing them as being 'a record of the times'. Despite the fact I could hardly understand his story with all its nautical jargon, it made me realise that one didn't have to be a learned person, nor one of any great experience, to keep a diary which could at a later date be transformed into a manuscript.

The boy's 19th century diary made good reading as well as good sense. It was then I decided if ever I made my first trip to sea, I would also keep occasional diaries. Then at a later date – a much later date – and if the opportunity arose, I would as my predecessor had, produce in some small way 'a record of the times'.

In the Sea School

In the Wellesley Nautical School we all wore Royal Navy rig and abided by the code of practice of the service. Many of the officers at the school had formerly served in the Senior Service, with the seamanship instructors having been Chief Petty Officers or Riggers. Many of the boys who attended the school, if proven to be of the required substance, were encouraged to join the Royal Navy and would be given special tuition or 'drafting routine' shortly before they left. They would then be sent to the shore training establishments of HMS *Ganges* or *Raleigh*. I was also in line to join the Royal Navy, but because of a favourable difference in pay between the services, as well as the more liberal freedom I'd heard of, I decided in the last few weeks of my schooling to enter the Merchant Navy.

When I left the sea school towards the end of May 1953 I'd just turned sixteen, was five feet one inch in height and weighed eight stone fully clothed.

The 'ship's tailor' in the sea school had made me a pin stripe utility suit on which he placed a value of 25/-. I also received a cardboard suitcase which resembled a leather one, in this I was to carry the bare essentials of clothing which were to give me a start in life.

From the coffers of the sea school I was given 5/- and a bus ticket from Blyth to North Shields; on my arrival there I was to report to a lodging house at 66 Law Road where I would stay until I joined my first ship.

The lodging house was often frequented by ex-Wellesley boys because of its cheap rate, and it was here I met Worms Worthington an old acquaintance who'd been in the sea school with me. My lodgings were free, however Worms, who'd already made a trip to sea, had to pay 6/- a week for his fare which included three meals a day. I'd often wondered why he'd been given the nickname of 'Worms', but on being asked he didn't know either and I assumed it was because he was tall and skinny.

Worms and I had always been good friends in the Wellesley where there were usually about a hundred boys aged between fourteen and sixteen. He was one of a large number at the sea school who were sent periodically from a Sheffield orphanage for a career at sea. I'd been sent there, like a few more, for non-compliance of school rules which in the main was non-attendance.

At the earliest opportunity, I registered at the Merchant Navy Establishment in South Shields where I was told to report each morning for a ship. I didn't know what kind of a ship I'd be given, I had no choice and even if I had it wouldn't have mattered as I couldn't tell one ship from another. A day or two went by while I enjoyed the fruits of a new life and the relative freedom of staying out late until 23h30. Worms and I were then told to report at the Merchant Navy Pool to join the Eagle Oil tanker *San Velino.* We were both excited at the prospect of being able to ship out together, where Worms could keep a watchful eye on me. Unfortunately we were to discover later on there'd been a mix up of names at the Pool, the result was I was excluded from joining the *San Velino,* and told I'd have to join one of the other available ships. The following day, which was a Friday, I was informed that on the Monday I was to join a ship called *Willesden* belonging to Watts Watts & Company of London.

First Look at a Ship

Having nothing better to do on the Saturday afternoon, Worms and I made our way to the riverbank on the North Shields side of the Tyne. We'd gone there just to have a look at this ship named *Willesden*, and which at the time was in John Redhead's repair yard at South Shields. Once there on the riverbank, Worms, who already had nine month's sea time, was to pass on his superior knowledge of shipping to me.

The only ships I'd ever seen in my life, were those I'd seen from the ferry on the River Mersey as well as the colliers at Blyth. The only big ships I'd ever seen in Blyth, were the *Adviser* belonging to T&J Harrison Lines which was under repair, and the *Clan Macnair* of The Clan Line which at the time was being broken up. While the Clan Line ship was being dismantled, we at the sea school had done a good job in salvaging much of the equipment on board. This included charts, bridge logs, rope, wire rope, paint, gratings and dozens of other items, all to be used in the sea school for the further advancement of future seamen.

Peace reigned over the industrious River Tyne on the sunny Saturday afternoon. The weekend had already begun and the deafening noise of the rivetters, sand blasters, and all the other shipyard bedlam had ceased. The river was strewn with ships of all shapes and sizes, on the buoys, alongside, or half built on the stocks; most were colliers which not only carried coal in their holds, but also burnt it to drive their steam engines. On this warm and windless day, such evidence of the coal burners was quite clear as thick black palls of smoke could be seen rising skywards from some of them. Their woodbine funnels, grimy black hulls, and buff upper works were evidence to the fact these vessels were not built for style or elegance.

However, after identifying all the ships in view, we were advised by a passer by we were in the wrong place.

Moving further along the banks, we at last came to a spot directly opposite Redheads shipyard, and it was there where I first caught sight of the *Willesden.* Riding high out of the water and standing out from all the other ships in the river, she lay alongside the repair jetty and appeared massive. Freshly painted all over with a grey hull, her upper works were a brilliant white, while her masts, derricks, and samson posts were a buff colour. The large expanse of red boot topping and her short black funnel gave her a distinctive but colourful identity from all the other grubby little vessels in the river. Her two masts were without topmasts, and a signal mast on the Monkey Island carried her house flag, this was plain white with the blue letter W in the centre. On her raised white focs'le and even from a distance, her name stood boldly out in contrasting black; the name of my first ship, *Willesden.*

"Well there she is," said Worms. "There's your first ship, and now you'll really find out what work is." I was silent as my eyes went over her deserted decks looking for something I could identify or relate to, unfortunately I knew nothing of ships, except maybe as I'd always thought, the more funnels a ship had the faster it would go.

In the sea school, we'd been taught about the sailing and racing of whalers and cutters at weekends. Then in the seamanship class during the week we'd practice rope and wire splicing, palm and needlework and loads of fancy knots and sennets. One day a week would be for signalling and navigation; then we had to learn all the Royal Navy procedures of marching up and down, saluting and ceremonial parades. Worms told me except for the rope work I'd learned from the rigger, just about everything else I'd been taught I may as well forget; in the MN there was never time – nor need – for all that square bashing and tiddly work.

As we sat on the riverbank I told Worms I was most impressed by the appearance of the *Willesden*, both in size and her immaculate paintwork. Worms told me whoever her bosun was would probably do his best to keep it so clean and this was one of the reasons I was to sign on the ship. He told me in my capacity as a deck boy I'd be paid £10 a month which worked out to ten pence an hour, or £2 - 6s - 8d for a fifty-six hour week, and for overtime I'd get 1/6d per hour. He also told me the Merchant Navy had recently been given a pay rise, and in my case, the pay of a deck boy had been increased from £9 to £10 a month, and the weekly working hours had been reduced from seventy, to fifty-six. I felt quite happy receiving such a good wage for working so few hours.

There were only two rates of overtime in the deck department: for able seamen it was 3/- whilst for ordinary seamen and deck boys it was 1/6.

Worms informed me the *Willesden* was an Empire Boat, just one of the many hundreds of such ships built during the WW2 emergency programme. "You'll see them in every port you go to," said Worms. "Such ships are easily identifiable." He then went on to say the British wartime shipbuilding effort had been mainly concentrated on 'Empire Boats' – so called because their names usually began with the prefix *Empire*. These vessels were of about 7,000 tons gross, and 10,000 tons deadweight with a speed of about ten or eleven knots (I was later to find out the *Willesden* had been built in 1944 as the *Empire Canning*). Worms continued by saying the Canadian war effort of building cargo ships consisted of 'Fort' and 'Park' Boats, whilst the Americans had constructed thousands of Liberty Ships which were otherwise referred to as 'Sam Boats'. The Yanks had also built numerous T2 tankers and latterly Victory Ships, both these latter types being capable of making fifteen knots. Worms warned me about ever sailing on a Liberty Ship because of their structural defects. "They've been known to break their backs," he continued, "and then go down before you can get your life jacket on."

I liked Worms, he was a real Yorkshire lad and being a year or so older than myself had already made a trip to sea. I felt quite sorry when we split up and he joined the *San Velino* as a JOS.

Worms told me in a way I was lucky, because the *San Velino* was to go up the 'Perishing' Gulf to Mena al Ahmadi. At the time of their arrival in June or July, the temperatures could be expected to be well over the one hundred degree mark and the heat even at night time would be almost unbearable. I told Worms I didn't care where the *Willesden* was going or for how long, and could hardly wait until Monday when I would sign on and find out. I knew the two days would drag before I could step on board and begin my sea career, anticipating all the delicious food I'd heard about.

In the sea school where we'd both spent two years of our lives, the food had been wholesome but lacking in quality. We always had sugarless porridge for breakfast, accompanied by three slices of bread with a pat of margarine hardly bigger than a half-crown. The main attraction of this feast would be a tablespoon of baked beans, jam, or a piece of cheese. The lunch prepared by Mr. Curry, an ex-army cook, was nearly always spuds, cabbage, carrots and gravy; then we'd have sago, tapioca, steam duff or some other pudding. At 17h00 we had teatime which was often an exact repeat of breakfast. Then at 20h00 we'd have either bread and dripping or hard tack with cocoa. Sunday was the day we looked forward to when we were each allocated a boiled or fried egg for breakfast; we had meat for lunch, and those who'd kept their dormitory the smartest were rewarded with a piece of cake at tea time. Nevertheless, each and every boy at the school had never been so well fed and complaints about the food were unheard of. There was one thing none of us could understand though – why did Miss Daulby the matron who received a fresh delivery of bread each morning, always keep it for two days before we were allowed to eat it? We all thought it was because she was trying to be strict or it may have been some form of punishment. Still, nobody ever dared to ask the reason why.

§

"D'you think you'll be seasick?" asked Worms, who'd already confessed to having suffered the indignity. "Because if you are, don't go on the weather side and get it all back in your face like I did." I laughed at the suggestion of being seasick, for that dreaded affliction was associated with rolling ships. "How can I be seasick on a ship so big?" I asked Worms. "Look at the size of her! She's far too big to roll." It was Worms's turn to laugh, "You'll see."

As I looked the half-mile or so over the River Tyne on the quiet Saturday afternoon, I saw movement on the deck of the *Willesden*. In the distance, the figure of a man could be seen walking from aft to amidships.

"Let's go on board and have a look around," I urged, however Worms assured me the gates to the shipyard would be locked, the man I'd just seen was probably the watchman; he was there to ensure no unauthorised persons boarded the vessel. I was also told the watchman would be responsible for tending to the berthing ropes as well as keeping a fire watch.

"You'll be rich on Monday," said Worms. "You can get an advance note and have a good time before you sail." He then went on to tell me most ships gave an advance of wages, and a sum of £1 or maybe even £2 might be forthcoming. He also told me the moneylender who cashed the advance note, was liable to deduct two shillings in the pound as his fee. This was good news to me, because all I had left out of my five shillings discharge money was half a crown. Worms told me not to spend it, because I'd have to pay that amount for my discharge book and passport photo on Monday. I was quite content sitting there on the banks of the Tyne observing the activity on the river, but Worms could see me gazing over at my first ship. He said once I was out in the Western Ocean or in the Bay of Biscay, my thoughts of a leisurely life at sea would quickly disappear.

After an hour or so of lazing around in which Worms educated me in the art of living on board ships, we made our way over to South Shields. He gave me a shilling saying I could repay him if I got an advance note, if not, then I could forget about it. He told me when I joined the ship, I would be entering a completely new way of life in comparison with the Wellesley Nautical School. In the school, every boy had to guard every single one of his possessions to the utmost, otherwise it would do a 'disappearing act'. On ships things were different, nobody used locks and everyone could leave their belongings in their locker without fear of it growing legs and doing the vanishing trick. He told me of one first tripper he'd heard about, who'd put a padlock on his locker. Later, when the first tripper entered the cabin he shared with three other shipmates, he found the lock had been broken off and was lying on the deck, not one of his possessions had been taken but the message was clear: locks are a sign of mistrust.

We went over to South Shields by ferry as I didn't want to miss out on anything. I wanted to see as much as I could and deep within me was a tremendous feeling of excitement. Worms pointed to an old warship on the South Shields side and informed me it was the HMS *Calliope*, a light cruiser which had taken part in the Battle of Jutland during the First World War.

Signing On

At 10h00 on Monday May 23 1953, I presented myself at the South Shields shipping office otherwise known as 'The Pool'. I wore my posh utility pinstripe suit, a shirt and tie and never looked smarter. My parade boots, absolutely gleaming, had been subjected to four hours of polishing for I knew today I would be seeing some important people and had no desire to be seen in an unfavourable light.

Within the 'signing on room' – actually a large hall – there was a gathering of well dressed men wearing collars and ties, most of them wearing either a trilby or a cloth cap while two or three boasted bowler hats. Just about everybody was smoking and a thick pall of smoke pervaded the room. Three ships were to sign on during the morning, and the men inside the hall were separated into groups for their respective ships. Worms had come along to offer his expert advice and showed me where to collect my discharge book for which I had to give my half-crown

Of those three groups within the hall, the *Willesden* was to sign on first. It was then I learned the ship was to sail in ballast to Montreal, load a full cargo of grain then return to the UK in a voyage which should take about five weeks. I waited in a formed line feeling a little nervous, the men in the queue with me were to be my shipmates, their accents were mostly Geordie and they all seemed to know each other. I felt very lost, then someone over the counter who probably noticed me in my nervous state called out as if it weren't obvious enough, "Who's the deck boy?" At last I had a title.

I moved forward through the smoke filled room and was warmly greeted by a gentleman who turned out to be the shipping master; at his side stood another well-dressed, bespectacled man wearing a brown suit who eyed me sternly. The shipping master showed me a huge sheet of yellowish paper with lots of small print on it known as the 'Articles of Agreement', he pointed out they were the conditions under which I would serve, be paid and fed. He further told me they were two-year articles, a voyage was always liable to last so long, however this voyage would only last a month or so. He asked me if I had any questions before signing, all I could say was I felt a bit disappointed at such a short voyage. He told me not to worry, I could always make another voyage on the same ship following its return to the UK. The important looking man next to him gave a measured smile and I wondered who he was. I was given a pen and directed to sign at the bottom of a list of deck department names. The shipping master was quite jovial, saying although I may be signing at the bottom of the list today, if I went about things the right way I could one day be signing at the top. He finished off by telling me the 'Articles' would be placed in some prominent position on the ship, probably the main alleyway, where each and every member of the crew could read and have access to them.

I failed to gather enough courage to ask him for an advance note in case he realised I was broke and asked me what I wanted the money for. However, he wished me the best of luck and asked me to move along the counter to another person who had a single gold band on his uniform sleeve. "Allotment or advance note?" he asked. I breathed a sigh of relief. Worms had told me to ask for £2, but once again my courage failed me – what if the officer asked what does a boy like me want with so much money? Maybe I should discard the advice of Worms and ask for £1. I could easily live for a week on so much, even two weeks, and with the ship sailing within the next few days who needs £2? "A pound sir, please," I mumbled to the pleasant looking gentleman, who I later discovered was Mr. Collister the third mate. "A pound?" he queried with a big smile on his face. "Who's going to cash an advance note of one pound? You better have two." Once again I had a feeling of relief within me and signed for a £2 advance note which I was to hand to the moneylender.

Making our exit from the shipping office an hour or so after entering, we found dozens of men gathered outside. Worms told me they were all sailors, firemen and stewards waiting for some ship or other to 'go through the pool'. He then pointed out another, smaller group of men on the street corner. In the centre of this group was a rather overweight man, cloth-capped and wearing a heavy gold watch and chain from his waistcoat pocket. He was the person to whom I was to give the advance note – the moneylender – and the heavy gold watch and chain were an advertisement of his wealth, prosperity and power. I gave the fat be-jowled man the advance note and he looked at me, or should I say he looked right through me, as if to form an opinion of my character. "Furst ship Hinney?" he inquired in his strong Geordie accent. I nodded in agreement. "Well," he said, "I hope you know I take two bob in the pound." His shifty eyes had a quick look around to ensure he wasn't about to be assailed, then from his inside pocket he drew a wallet crammed with notes. From one side he peeled off a £1 note, from the other side a 10/- note, then three florins from somewhere else. He gave me the princely sum of 36/- saying, "I'll bet you've never had that much money in your life have you Hinney?" I agreed and took the money. "D'you know," he went on, "most lenders I know take half a crown in the pound, and three bob for first trippers." He turned around asking his bodyguard of cronies who appeared to be ever on hand, "Ain't that right boys?" They agreed as one, telling me how lucky I was to be let off so light at ten per cent. The moneylender appeared to want to create some further amusement. "That's why I'm so poor – only taking two bob in the pound." The roar of laughter from his entourage of 'yes' men was immediate. I could see his side of the joke and appreciated his good humour. In his mirth, his body was shaking like a giant whale.

I turned to go away, but was tapped on the shoulder by the overweight moneylender. His cronies fell silent as he brought his face close to mine, looking me straight in the eye. His eyes went as hard as diamonds as he hissed, "Hinney, you make sure you're on that ship of yours when she goes down the river, won't you!" I assured him I would and made my departure.

Worms my guide and mentor refused to take back the shilling he'd lent me; later on told me how the advance note system worked. There was nothing new in it, in fact it had been going on for over a hundred years. After signing on, a seaman would request an advance of wages; the shipping company would oblige by giving him a company certificate with the amount of the advance written on it. The seaman would then take the certificate, or advance note, to a third party who would exchange it for the sum written on it, less any commission they may wish to charge. The size of the commission is of no consequence to the shipping company, it is an agreement between lender and borrower and the fee is normally ten per cent. The new owner of the advance note, the moneylender, will then send the advance note back to the shipping company, who in return will send back the full amount by cheque. "Unfortunately," said Worms, "if the seaman to whom the advance note is made fails to join the ship, the shipping company won't pay out and the moneylender is left high and dry with a worthless cancelled advance note." My mind wandered back to the moneylender's last words to me, "Hinney, you make sure you're on that ship of yours when she goes down the river, won't you!"

I'd been told to report on board after lunch. It took me no time at all to have my case packed and I happily said my good-byes to those in the lodging house. Worms, who'd offered to accompany me, told me I could arrive in style by getting a taxi right to the ship's gangway, and it would only cost about two shillings. I was horrified. "Only two shillings?" I gasped – to me two shillings was nothing short of a small fortune. I'd never been in a taxi in my life before and told Worms I was quite used to walking. I reminded him of the many occasions in the sea school when we'd all gone for a five mile route march before breakfast 'marching in step', and a ten mile 'march easy' on weekend afternoons. Worms suggested I should stop equating with the sea school, adding that maybe I was institutionalised and ought to start living a normal life. I thought about what he said and agreed, but I still wasn't going to hire a taxi for a journey of two miles or less. What if somebody on the ship saw me getting out of the taxi then discovered I'd travelled such a short distance? I would then no doubt be the subject of unfavourable conversation on the ship.

Joining the Ship

Worms wasn't due to sign on the *San Velino* until the next day, and as we walked through the tunnel to Readhead's yard, we spoke of both ships. I was given a grim picture of what lay in store for me with regard to the work I'd have to do; of sailing light ship across the Atlantic Ocean and all the new things I'd quickly have to learn. Making our way through the shipyard, we approached the *Willesden* from her after end where she lay starboard side to the quay. I stopped for a moment then put my cardboard case down to have a good look at her. The draught markings on the stern frame indicated there was nine feet of ship under water, whilst the markings went right up to thirty-one feet. I observed the huge propeller blades sticking up out of the dirty water with oil, newspapers, and loads of dunnage swirling around; on the ship's stern was her name and port of registry, '*Willesden* – London.'

"Look how light she is," exclaimed Worms as he pointed to the huge expanse of ship's side showing more boot topping than grey. "I wouldn't like to go across the Western on that thing, you'll be as sick as a pig." He told me the tanker he was to join could fill its tanks with sea water to minimise rolling, but I was probably in for a rough ride. Once again I repeated to Worms what I'd been told: a ship the size of the *Willesden* was far too big to roll, and once again he laughed at me. He pointed to a row of portholes above on the starboard side aft. This was where the sailor's accommodation would be. I walked forward past the gangway and was soon under the focs'le head, the deck of which must have been fifty or sixty feet from the water. There I noticed that the draught marks only went up to seven feet but I couldn't see the next draught marking of six feet because the water was so dirty with a thick layer of oil on it.

Worms advised me to hurry up, the bosun might be awaiting my arrival and he might be a swine like the last one he'd sailed with. We walked up the long gangway inscribed with John Readhead's name on its side. A section of the ship's guard-rails had been removed and the gangway rested on the ship's deck. On reaching the main deck, I stopped momentarily to have a look at the surroundings which were to be my next home. The steel decks had recently been painted in the same colour as the boot topping, the hatches were all battened down, the derricks lowered, and everything looked so neat and clean. I supposed all first trippers have that strange feeling at the point of boarding their first ship, and no less me. I stepped off the gangway and onto the ship, noticing how very quiet it was. It appeared there was nobody on board.

Worms told me I must find the bosun, and if he wasn't aboard, then the 1st mate, otherwise known as the chief officer. We made our way aft which according to my mentor would be the bosun's most likely place of abode. I was just about to step over the coaming into the after accommodation, when I heard a voice from behind, "Who are you son?" I turned around to be confronted by a stockily built man about five foot six inches tall with a pair of shoulders like an ox, his red face and black hair putting me in mind of a farmer. "I'm the new deck boy, sir, and I'm looking for the bosun."

"That's me, I'm the bosun," he said in his West Country accent, "and you don't have to call me sir." He seemed to consider this for a second before he said, "But when I deservedly get knighted by the Queen, then you can call me sir."

I didn't know whether to laugh or not.

The bosun was named Sam Barter and he told me he came from Bristol. He guided me down the companionway to the seamen's accommodation where I had my first little injury on a ship, as my head received a terrific bang on top of the low doorway. I then became aware of the smell of fresh paint mingled with the heat of the accommodation. This wasn't exactly an unpleasant smell but proved all the accommodation as well as the decks had been freshly painted. The bosun then showed me to a cabin on the starboard side which I was to share with Fred Hodges the lamp trimmer, who according to the bosun was a nice guy and came from Port Said. The two of us would be day workers. "Now, get your working gear on," said the bosun. "I'll be back for you in five minutes."

Worms told me I would no doubt be put to work until 18h00, but the good thing about it was I would be paid a full day's pay of 6/8d. He said he would see me in the coffee bar at 8 pm if I could get ashore. That was the last time I was ever to see Worms Worthington and after all the time we'd known each other, I never knew his first name. I don't think he knew mine either.

The cabin, about nine feet square and six feet ten inches high, looked quite comfortable with two bunks in it. The one the bosun had told me to occupy was more or less in the centre while my cabin mate had the inboard one. There were two drawers under each of the bunks and a steel locker each for a suit, raincoat etc. There were two brass portholes in the ship's side with the glass in each almost an inch thick. The steel deck in the cabin was covered by a couple of coir carpet runners. Over the doorway to the cabin was an inscription that read 'Certified Two Seamen'.

The bosun returned after a short while and quickly ascertained my birthplace by half stating, half inquiring, "You're a scouse aren't you?" When I agreed, he told me he'd been to Liverpool many times and told me of a number of public houses he'd frequented and began to name a few. He said he'd sailed with lots of scousers over the years and was glad to have me aboard. As he was speaking I couldn't help noticing the size of his fists and forearms. I just hoped I would never offend him enough to receive a crack over the lughole.

He then told me he'd been informed of my signing on and as this was my first trip to sea I was to be the mess boy, otherwise known as the peggy. He had me follow him up to the focs'le head, gave me buckets, scrubbing brushes, soap, polish, and cleaning rags then introduced me to my daily chores. The bosun appeared quite friendly and asked me if I'd ever seen the Liver Buildings on Liverpool's Pier Head.

"Of course I have, you can't help seeing them," I replied.

"Well d'you know the story about those Liver Birds on the top," he inquired.

"What about them?" I asked.

"Well," said the bosun, "if a virgin ever walks underneath them, they'll fly away." He then roared with laughter.

I was taken to the mess room on the starboard side amidships where upon entering I once more banged my head. The mess room was about twenty-eight by twelve feet, and I was told it had to be scrubbed out every single day. "Shipshape and Bristol fashion, on hands and knees," the bosun went on. He told me mops were strictly forbidden, and I must never be found in possession of one. "Only stewards and old women use mops," he informed me.

In the mess room there were seven tables, five of which were three-seaters spread around the sides of the compartment while in the centre were two four-seaters. There were two entrances into the mess room, and two long carpet runners stretched the length of the compartment. In the pantry, adjacent to the mess room and galley, was a big hot press over which were plate racks on the bulkhead. These racks were so designed that their contents couldn't, or were not supposed to, roll out. In both the mess room and the pantry were six brass portholes and judging by the fact they were absolutely green, hadn't been polished for a very long time. The pantry had a double drainer sink with drawers and cleaning gear lockers underneath, and as well as the mess room itself, had at all times to be kept in pristine condition. I was then introduced to the ship's cook and shown the galley and the range which was coal fired. I was told I had to regularly check the coal bin on the boat deck, and at all times I must keep the galley supplied with water. The running water to the galley was gravity fed from a tank on the boat deck directly above. To keep this tank topped up, I was to operate a handle on the main deck outside the galley, this pumped water up from the fresh water tanks in the number four 'tween deck. Next I was shown the after accommodation, this included the bathroom, toilets and showers, the recreation room, table tennis room and the alleyways down below, all of which had to be scrubbed out every day. The portholes and other brass work all had to be brought up to standard and then kept gleaming.

I was pleasantly surprised to find the ship had a table tennis room; the bosun told me under normal circumstances merchant ships wouldn't have such a luxury but this ship had been built during the war and the compartment had originally been designed as the gunner's cabin.

It seemed to me the tasks I'd been given were relatively easy, if this was all I had to do, but of course there was more – an awful lot more. I had to acquire the dry stores from the second steward every morning, the tea, sugar, and coffee, and I was responsible for making brews at the appropriate times. Then I must collect the bread from the cook who kept it in the fridge down below, after which I had to help with the preparation of all meals and do all the washing-up. Although no difficult manual task was involved in the collection of the dry stores and it may have sounded simple, I was later to find that it was my most annoying and time consuming job.

Soon after, the nine remaining members of the deck crowd arrived on board. They consisted of six able seamen and three ordinary seamen who were to be the watch keepers. We were all told on the following day the ship was to undergo engine trials and compass adjustments, then if successful, we would be sailing for Montreal as soon as possible. I found the crowd very friendly, and on learning I was making my first trip to sea, they offered every encouragement.

By now it was nearly 17h00 and I was made busy preparing the mess room for teatime. It didn't take me long to find out about some more of my chores, which included doing the peggying for the bosun, ten seamen, the carpenter, and six engine room greasers. While I was making tea in the two gallon teapot, I was witness to a spectacular argument between the bosun and the second steward. Apparently the second steward had informed the bosun the dining room was not a mess room but a cafeteria, and as the stewards would be using it, a waiter should be responsible for attending on them. The bosun exploded and told him the stewards must do their own cleaning up, the peggy was a first tripper and already had eighteen men to look after. The argument continued until they both went up to see the first mate to obtain his ruling; the bosun must have won, because later on he told me not to peggy on the stewards.

When 17h00 came it was teatime and I was to have my first meal on a ship. It was something I'd looked forward to for a long time and as usual I was starving. The cook had given me two long loaves to slice, it was lovely and fresh and my mouth was watering as I cut the bread. There were also plates of lovely green lettuce, tomatoes, cold potatoes, salad cream and a huge tray of sliced roast beef. On top of all that there was real butter. I had to pinch myself in case I was dreaming. The deck and engine crowd then came along and helped themselves while I filled their pint pots with tea. Eventually, and when they were all seated and eating, I was invited by one of the greasers to take a plate and help myself. I rather timidly took a small portion of each salad with a small slice of beef and sat in the corner of the mess room as quiet as a mouse. "What's the matter peggy, got no appetite?" asked one of the sailors, who having observed the amount of food I'd humbly helped myself to, could see my dilemma. Taking my plate he strode over to the table and heaped it high with salad and beef before placing it in front of me. "Think you can put that away?" he smiled. I happily affirmed I could, much to the approval and laughter of everyone around.

I'd heard for a long time about the good standard of food on board ships, but now, I was absolutely astounded. After I'd downed the plateful of food, I relaxed a little to let the best meal of my life go down. I made a comment to the greaser next to me who agreed on what a marvellous meal it had been; he told me Watts Watts & Company were noted for their good conditions. However, he went on, some shipping companies were so mean and hungry they had difficulties getting crews, and because of their bad name, no self-respecting seamen would go near them. He continued by saying such companies usually relied on employing men who couldn't get a ship, or employed men who'd been on the beach for a while or even men who had a poor record of discharges in their books. He further told me there'd been a big queue at the pool trying to sign on the *Willesden*.

I thought the meal was over and had begun collecting the plates and cutlery, when from the galley the cook shouted "Peggy!" I was in like a flash to see how I could repay him for preparing such a wonderful meal. I was absolutely flabbergasted when he pointed to a large tray full of ice cream and peaches. He told me to take it into the pantry and dole it out on dessert dishes for those who wanted it. Only the chippy and a couple more wanted any – I couldn't believe it! All that ice cream and nobody in the mess room to eat it.

After the meal the sailors and greasers were all lounging around smoking and making their acquaintances. The bosun, who was seated with Fred my cabin mate and the chippy, suddenly shouted from the after end of the mess room, "Hey scouse! I'll bet you can't eat all the ice cream and peaches what's left in the tray." Someone else then remarked if it wasn't eaten quickly, it would melt and would have to be emptied down the scupper. The mess went quiet awaiting my reply, "I'll bet you I can." There was a roar of approval. The tray was still almost full with sixteen or so helpings of ice cream remaining. Just then, the chippy who was an Estonian named Achmid Wichmann came up for a second helping, the abuse he received from the bosun was indescribable. The air was absolutely blue, and what he called the poor chippy cannot be repeated. Apparently, the bosun had on some previous occasion been shipmates with the chippy or knew of him. The bosun was aware of the chippy's alleged ravenous appetite and soon let everybody in the mess know about it. He also made a comment that any farmer would gladly keep the chippy in his field just for his droppings.

The bosun then came over and placed the ice cream tray in front me saying said he'd just bet a beer on me clearing the tray and that if he lost the bet, sparks would fly and I'd be in for it. I could hear a little voice inside my head laughing and telling me not only could I eat all the contents of the tray, but a lot more. By now, a few of the crowd had gathered around my table to observe and offer their encouragement. 'If only the boys in the sea school could see me now,' I thought as I got stuck in with a tablespoon. Within a few minutes the tray was devoid of its contents and I was given a standing ovation. One of the sailors, Bill Houston, whispered in my ear saying I should lick the tray for good measure. This I did, finishing with a huge burp sending Jock Niven, another of the sailors, into peals of laughter. Later on Bill Houston told me Jock Niven was a North Sea Chinaman and explained Jock was from the Shetland Islands where in times gone by, the people were noted for working without pay and for their food alone – hence the name.

As I began to wash up the plates and cutlery the bosun showed me how to economise on soap which, like everything else, must not be wasted. From the galley he fetched an empty two pound jam tin and made a lot of holes in it with his marlin spike. He then cut a block of soap into pieces and placed them in the jam tin, hanging it by a piece of seizing wire from the hot water tap. Any water that would now come from the tap would have to pass through the tin and make the water in the sink nice and soapy.

I'd also been given four tea towels from the second steward which were to be washed each evening and allowed to dry overnight in the pantry. These would be changed weekly when I would be given a further issue of soap and toiletries

Later on, the crowd who'd also received advance notes, made their way to the nearest watering hole. I was quite content to stay aboard cleaning up, as well as making a load of beef sandwiches for the crew's return. We all slept aboard as the ship would be putting to sea the next morning. The late supper was awaiting the sailors on their return after the pubs had closed, and so ended my first, and very happy, working day on board a ship.

§

I didn't need the watchman to wake me the next morning, in fact I hardly slept; up at first light, I decided to take a walk around the ship whilst everybody still slept. Inside the galley there was a clock on the bulkhead which could be seen through a peephole in the galley door, and I could see it was 04h45. Everything was so quiet as I went exploring my new maritime home – on the focs'le, along the boat deck and around the poop deck, under the focs'le – where the chippy had his workshop and Fred Hodges had his lamp room, paint store and rope store. I noticed everything was locked up. Just then a loaded collier named *Tudor Queen* went steaming past and out to sea; judging by the smoke coming from her woodbine funnel it must have been a coal burner. I was glad I wasn't on the little *Tudor Queen* as it only had about two feet of freeboard and I could imagine the sea rushing over her decks in any kind of weather.

Deciding to venture down onto the quayside I was amazed to see the draught markings had changed dramatically. On the stern frame they'd gone to seventeen feet and on the stem fourteen feet. This I later discovered was because the chippy had filled the deep tanks in number four hold with ballast water in readiness for when the ship put to sea.

Back on board I pumped up the water to the galley for the next twenty minutes and checked the contents of the coal bunker. By now it was 06h30, time for the crowd to show their faces, and I was unsure whether or not I should make a big pot of tea. I made it anyway.

When they arrived in the mess room the looks on their faces could not have been more different from the night before. Instead of high spirits, the mess room was deathly quiet. Some of them were holding their heads in their hands as they sat at the tables sipping their tea. One crew member said he would never drink beer again.

Crew List of the MV *Willesden* – signed on at South Shields on May 23rd 1953
Number of crew 39

Voyage from South Shields to Montreal

Name	Rank	Age	Address	Monthly Wage	Last Ship
FW Grist	Master	48	Berkshire	?	*Twickenham*
J Kirby	1st Mate	26	Newport	£52-10	*Woodford*
O Brown	2nd Mate	27	Edinburgh	£42-0	*Beckenham*
J Collister	3rd Mate	24	Hornchurch	£33-15	*Beckenham*
G Chell	Apprentice	19	Stroud	£ 8-0	?
A Brown	Radio Officer	57	Melbourne	£38-0	*Nurjehan*
A Wichmann	Carpenter	57	Estonia	£33-10	*Wanstead*
S Barter	Bosun	27	Bristol	£31-5	*Twickenham*
J Coyne	AB	32	South Shields	£28-0	*Lady Charrington*
J Fahy	AB	28	Galway	£25-0	*Cormull*
R Atmore	AB	23	Grimsby	£26-0	*Barford*
W Houston	AB	28	Hebburn on Tyne	£28-0	*Norton*
C Slater	AB	30	Grimsby	£28-0	*British Talent*
F Hodges	AB - Lamptrimmer	29	Portishead	£28-0	*Twickenham*
E Merson	SOS	20	Portroy	£18-0	*Pine Hill*
J Edmund	SOS	19	South Shields	£18-0	*Norton*
A Egan	JOS	18	South Shields	£15-10	*Regent Lion*
J Niven	AB	33	Shetlands	£28-0	*Boscombe*
J Richardson	Deck Boy	16	Liverpool	£10-0	(First Ship)
E Duncan	Chief Engineer	59	W. Lothian	£82-10	*Beckenham*
D Stirling	2nd Eng.	26	Wallsend	£52-10	*Woodford*
J Murray	3rd Eng.	28	Greenock	£36-15	*Kadiek*
M Lewis	4th Eng.	21	Glamorgan	£30-0	*Willesden*
W Gibson	Jnr. Eng.	21	Glasgow	£28-0	*Kalewa*
G Fagan	Jnr.Eng.	23	Old Penshaw	£28-0	*Pompey Light*
R Collins	Jnr. Eng.	21	Barry	£28-0	*Wendover*
A Leonard	D. Greaser	61	Durham	£30-5	*Beckenham*
G Mcintosh	D. Greaser	46	Glasgow	£30-5	*Wave Baron*
A Hale	D Greaser	39	North Shields	£30-5	*Empire Mead*
W Orbell	D Greaser	55	Kirby	£30-5	*Baltara*
W Gibson	D Greaser	30	Grimsby	£30-5	*Baron Yarborough*
J Chafer	D Greaser	34	Barton	£30-5	*Baltara*
J Perkins	Chief Stwd.	52	Cardiff	£37-10	*Greenwich*
J Profit	2nd Stwd.	22	South Shields	£27-10	*Polar Maid*
J Bartnett	Asst Stwd.	23	South Shields	£27-0	*Ormonde*
J Kendal	Ship's Cook	32	Newport	£34-10	*B.P. Refiner*
H Grogan	2nd Cook Baker	21	South Shields	£28-10	*Gryfevale*
R Housby	Cabin Boy	17	South Shields	£10-0	*Waynegate*
S Fowler	Cabin Boy	18	South Shields	£10-0	*Wokingham*

Sea Trials

The bosun, who was very nimble for his weight, was up and about and turned the hands to at 07h00. We were supposed to sail at 09h00 and I couldn't keep still. All the sailors were on day work and the ship was due to return to South Shields after the sea trials, which should be before teatime. The ship, I was told, had been laid up for a few months and the magnetic compasses were expected be a long way out of true.

The ship didn't have a gyrocompass and it didn't have radar either, these modern navigation aids were very expensive and I'd been told by Paddy Fahy that radar cost £4000. During the ship's long stay in South Shields, the engines having been completely overhauled, would also require a thorough testing. The bosun lined up all the sailors on the afterdeck detailing them off for their sea watches and stations for entering and leaving port. He said he wanted the *Willesden* 'Shipshape and Bristol fashion' but I suppose he was just saying that to let everyone know where he came from. I was observing and listening to the boson's opening speech and couldn't help noticing, as all the sailors stood there in their shirt sleeves that unlike the shore people, there wasn't an ounce of fat on any one of them. The sailors each carried a sheath in their belt which had a knife and a marlin spike in it, while Jock Niven also carried a pair of pliers in his. Breakfast time came at 08h00 and while I was collecting the plates, the bosun made an announcement. He informed everyone in the mess room that in future they must scrape their own plates into the gash bucket then leave them in the sink, this was obviously for my benefit and to lighten my work load a bit.

By this time I'd managed to bang my head six times when passing through doorways, and the last bump I'd received had left me bleeding. Each contact of my head with a doorway left a lump and I was jokingly advised to wear a miner's safety helmet. Everybody assured me I would soon get used to the doorways. Considering I was the smallest person on the ship, it just went to show how low these entrances were. At first I would dash through these doorways until, after watching the others and taking stock, I noticed they would first pause, then stoop automatically before ducking through the opening.

The sailors were divided into two groups for entering and leaving port – which were otherwise known as 'stations'. One half was on the focs'le with Mr. Kirby the first mate and the bosun, the other half were aft with Mr. Brown the second mate and the lamp trimmer Fred Hodges. The bosun told me I needn't go on stations and my time would be better spent finishing off my work and getting 'smoko' ready.

At 09h00 I was in the pantry when the telegraph from the bridge to the engine room sounded with a jangling of bells. This was followed by a bang of compressed air coming from the engine room resulting in the ship's engines shuddering into life. As I assumed we were pulling away from the quayside, I ran out onto the deck to see the ship move away, however there was no movement as the ship was still alongside. The telegraph sounded again and again and the engines stopped and started. At times the engines were going faster, but the ship still didn't move. I then noticed, quite puzzled, all the berthing ropes were still made fast, holding the ship to the quay. When the sailors came in for their coffee at smoko time, they told me this was just an engine trial, and we'd be sailing at 11h00hrs. When the crowd returned to stations after their smoko, a tug arrived and was secured to the port shoulder. The tug was a coal burner with a tall woodbine funnel and the smoke from it blew right across the focs'le head over the coughing sailors who were stationed there.

Needless to say, not much work was performed on my behalf during the morning, as I was so busy asking people questions and trying to find out what was going on. Looking from the pantry doorway I saw George Chell, the apprentice, haul down the Blue Peter flag then hoist the pilot flag to take its place. Shortly afterwards I heard a powerful voice coming from the bridge, "Let go forrard." Followed by, "Let go aft." The bridge telegraph conveyed its message to the engine room, and the engines came to life.

The propeller thrashed the water which changed colour from a dirty brown to a dirty green, and the ship moved away from her berth. The tug then guided its charge out into the middle of the river, the engines stopped and the ship turned around to starboard. Once again the engines came to life, and the *Willesden* proceeded down river past the pier and out into the North Sea. The pilot disembarked onto the tug, which was then let go and my first taste of sea life had begun.

As soon as I had the chance I went up on the boat deck and stood over the galley, from there I had a better view of the grey North Sea as it swished past. When I'd first seen the ship, I'd imagined she would glide swiftly and silently through the water, but I was so wrong! The engines were making a fearful racket as they drove the ship along, and looking down the fidley, I wondered how anybody could work down in the engine room with so much noise going on. On the bridge I could see there was a lot of activity; two bowler-hatted men were on the monkey island looking in at the compass binnacle and relaying messages to someone else on the bridge wing (I later found out that these were the compass correctors). It was quite cold on the boat deck, so I went down aft to put my coat on. I could feel the ship vibrating a lot as I walked aft, down below in the accommodation the ship was actually rattling, and the noise from the steering gear flat didn't improve matters. I saw Old George McIntosh, one of the greasers, coming out of the steering gear compartment, and asked him was the ship always going to be as noisy as this. He told me not to worry because I'd get used to it in a day or so. He showed me a big steel quadrant in the middle of the steering flat and told me directly beneath this was the rudder. As I watched the quadrant move with a clattering hiss of steam, George told me it was the helmsman who'd caused the movement as he applied the wheel. Old George then went on to tell me when the ship was fully loaded, the propeller would be so far under water it would hardly be heard. Apparently, a helmsman who used excessive wheel, which moved the quadrant, wouldn't make himself very popular with those who lived aft.

Lunch time came and once again there was a lovely meal of roast spuds, cabbage and lamb chops, with steam duff and custard for afters. I left nothing on my plate and this was observed by the bosun who called me a little gannet. He claimed I was nearly as bad as the chippy who also scraped his plate clean. After lunch we were out of sight of land, but when I excitedly mentioned this to those who passed by they didn't seem interested in the slightest. I spent a lot of time during the day looking out to sea and feeding the seagulls on the dinner leftovers; I thought at the same time if those birds had to rely on the remains of my food they'd soon starve to death. I didn't make the best job of my allotted work during the day and this was noticed by the bosun who reminded me in no uncertain terms I was here to work and was not a passenger.

It was 16h00 by the time we returned to South Shields and I found it difficult to accept how noisy the ship could be. The engine itself sounded like a rickety old typewriter; the steering gear compartment bothered me with its hissing clackety quadrant; the propeller made a horrible crackling noise and then there was the terrible vibrating. Another thing I couldn't understand, was why Fred Hodges – who'd had the pick of all the cabins – chose the one next to the steering gear flat. Well, I suppose if nobody else was worried about such a fearful din, then why should I be? As Old George had said, I'd get used to it in a day or two. Apparently the engine trials had been a success, the compasses were corrected and the ship was to sail for Montreal in two days time.

The teatime meal consisted of cottage pie which was absolutely delicious – thankfully, there were plenty of leftovers. By the time I'd finished, however, there was no wastage. Once again the bosun had a laugh at me making comments about my appetite but I informed him it was a sin to waste food and I was a most devout person with not a sin upon my soul. "What about the sin of greed?" he asked.

I wasn't used to this level of work but fortunately for me after teatime I had the advantage of being able to take my time doing the cleaning up. I didn't go ashore even though I still had the 36/- in my pocket. Maybe I was worried if when I tried to return, the ship might have gone.

The following day there were a lot of victuals to be taken on board. The deck crowd manned the derricks and drove the winches at number three hatch, and with the use of a cargo net all the stores were soon piled up on the deck. The stewards took theirs down below to the storeroom which was situated beneath the chief engineer's cabin on the main deck of the bridge. Then came the deck and engine room stores and all day everybody was busy preparing the ship to sail.

Sailing Day

I was up early the next morning to see the last minute preparations being made for sailing, which was to be after breakfast time. The Blue Peter and the ship's international code of signals were flying from the signal mast on the monkey island, and as usual there was a seagull perched on the truck.

On May 27 at 09h00 we let go from South Shields with the same pilot but a different tug. I noticed as we went past the breakwater, one of the greasers was waving to a woman who was waiting there. He later told me each time he left South Shields his mother would wait to wave him off no matter what the weather was like and even if he was down below, she never missed the opportunity. Soon the ship was out at sea and the tug had been let go, but before the pilot went with it one of the stewards gave him some letters to post. The ship went out a couple of miles then altered course to port heading north. An hour or so later Blyth lighthouse could be seen in the distance on the port side. During my stay at the sea school in Blyth, I had with the rest of the lads often sat on the beach watching the collier ships entering and leaving the port. Sometimes away in the distance, a ship could be seen heading north or south. Of those amongst us, the 'experts' would sometimes identify one of these as a foreign going vessel. As the ship would slowly move out of visibility, we would discuss the ship and feel some envy for those on board. We would talk about their pay and conditions, the cheap duty-free cigarettes they enjoyed, and of course the food they ate. We spoke of the day which would one day arise, when any one of us may be on one of those distant ships. Today my turn had come and I wondered if any boys were watching from the beach discussing the foreign going ship on the horizon.

During lunchtime, the word went around a bond issue was to be given and we could buy duty-free cigarettes. Capstan, Senior Service, and Players were 8/- for a 200 carton, Export Woodbines 6/6d for 200, a four ounce tin of Capstan 7/6d, while a four ounce tin of Justmans was 4/10d.

I don't really know why I smoked, maybe it's because in the sea school cigarettes were such a prized asset. In the school one of the many little rackets which went on was conducted by the tobacco barons and most of the trading involved food. Some of the deals on hand allowed you to get a roll up for your pudding, or two roll ups for your Sunday morning egg. Of all the smoking requisites in that school, tailor made cigarettes were the greatest luxury. There were various other bargains on hand, but food was always the most popular currency. I never, ever swopped my rations with anyone for the simple reason I thought more of my food than I did of tobacco. Another reason was I'd once observed two of these tobacco barons mixing tobacco with dried horse manure from the coalman's horse.

At the bond issue I treated myself to 200 Woodbines, but it wasn't quite so easy. The chief steward who was on the other side of the serving hatch eyed me first, then asked if I wasn't a bit too young to smoke. He had a cockney accent, spoke very fast, and had a pair of eyes like a jackdaw (or like the moneylender in South Shields). I told him I only smoked a couple of cigarettes a day – thereby catching myself in my own trap. "Oh," exclaimed the chief. "If you only smoke two a day, then all you need is one packet of twenty each week. So if I let you have a carton it will last you three months, so I'll see you at the end of August." After amusing all the people in the queue he relented. "OK scouse," he went on in a voice that sounded like a burst of machine gun fire, "sign here for six and a tanner."

After the bond issue we had lifeboat drill, I was in boat number two where Mr. Kirby the first mate would take command if the time came. Later we had fire drill where one of the sailors had to get dressed up in a fearnought suit and the fire hydrants and the hoses were all tested.

Fred Hodges was my cabin mate, he was about six feet tall and on speaking to him I found he was from Portishead near Bristol and not Port Said as I'd thought the bosun had said. Just like all the other sailors he seemed very friendly and easy to get on with. He was the lamp trimmer, and when I asked him how he got a title like that, he told me it was the name normally bestowed on the man who was next senior to the bosun. Fred told me the origins of the name lamp trimmer came from long ago and was given to the person who would tend the oil lamps on ships of sail. The name continued with the passage of time, although the lighting in ships was now powered by electricity. He also told me the peggy got his name from the days of the old men-o'-war, when one of the peg legged sailors was given the relatively easy task of keeping the mess deck clean

At about 18h30, after I'd washed up, I went down aft to feed the seagulls. I had a rather stale loaf and was breaking lumps off it casually tossing them up into the air. I was really enjoying myself until I heard an enraged scream from behind; it came from the second cook who was also the baker. "I'm the one who has to bake this bread you little birdbrain," he roared at me. "Don't ever let me catch you wasting my bread again or you'll be getting fed to the seagulls yourself – in mincemeat form." I tried to apologise, but he took off back to the galley. However I found out the bread I'd been giving to the birds was shore bread, a huge consignment of which had been delivered to the ship on sailing day and had not been baked on board. It later transpired, even after five days, we were still eating this same shore bread which had by now started to go mouldy and only after several complaints did the second cook make fresh bread for the first time. As the new batch was being baked, I saw the cabin boy throwing the remainder of the shore bread over the wall.

Being summertime it went dark quite late, but long before the sun went down all the other sailors had either gone on watch at 20h00 or turned in. I eventually got into my bunk and attempted to sleep, however the vibration of the ship, the hissing clackety-clack of the steering gear and then the propeller made it impossible. I never did sleep that night, although the noise didn't appear to bother my cabin mate Fred one bit and I just couldn't work out why he hadn't grabbed one of the forward cabins where it was quieter. I was shortly to find out.

The next morning I was up at 04h30, shortly before dawn. It was pointless staying in my bunk unable to sleep and I thought I might just as well make an early start on my work amidships.

I felt very tired, but on venturing out on the deck the fresh air wakened me a little. I had a quick look down the engine room at the diesels thumping away. Old Bill Orbell was about to go down below and I asked him if he would show me the engine room. I was given a grand tour and was even allowed down the shaft tunnel. There I was surprised to find it took only 90 rpm on the propeller shaft to push the ship along. Afterwards I went back up on the next engine room deck and watched the huge pistons all moving differently. There was nobody around so I decided to have a walk up to the focs'le head, but when I got halfway up the foredeck, I heard someone calling me from behind. It was the first mate, Mr. Kirby, who summoned me to the bridge.

When I arrived he asked me why I was wandering around at such an early hour and I told him that I hadn't slept all night. Just like everyone else, he told me, I'd have to get used to the ship. I was then told by the chief officer to keep off the decks at such an odd hour. Going into the mess room I tried to catch a few minutes sleep with my head on one of the tables when the lookout came down from the focs'le. When I told him I hadn't slept with all the noise down aft, he just said, "Don't worry you'll get used to it."

In the lovely sunny morning before turning to, I stood aft for a while watching the propeller churning up the water as the ship headed up the North Sea. Later on I felt like a wet rag as I laboured through the day. I could feel the eyes of the bosun upon me – the type of eyes which never missed a trick. I felt he was in a happier mood when we were in port and wondered if it was because there were public houses on hand. I'd also taken note of the fact, when I was on the receiving end of a frequent scolding, I was 'peggy' or 'hey you' but when he was in a better mood he addressed me as 'scouse'. If this was in some way a sign of good will, then maybe Fred the lampy had more understanding – he always called me as 'scouse'. At sea, the bosun was always alert and I was surprised at his nimbleness – he wasn't fat but very solid and could have been taken for a weight lifter. In fact there were no fat people on the ship, except for Mr. Perkins the chief steward.

My first scolding of the day came from the bosun when I emptied a bucket of dirty water over the side amidships, this resulted in some of it blowing back over the white painted bulwarks. Afterwards he told me that in future all gash must be dumped from aft, going on to say that another lazy deck boy he knew had thrown an old wire rope over the wall from amidships. The wire rope had finished up in the propeller and the ship had to be towed into port costing the company hundreds of pounds. After hearing this I never, ever threw anything overboard from amidships – unless of course I knew for certain the bosun was on the focs'le.

I then saw Achmid the chippy carrying a length of line with pieces of metal attached to it. He put chalk on the metal parts before lowering the implement down a pipe. I was soon to find out that he was taking soundings of the bilges and the fresh water tanks. The 'implement' he was using was a 'sounding rod'.

Later in the day after I'd gone through the motions of working, I went into the recreation room aft where the noise wasn't as bad. I'd decided that after 20h00, this was where I'd head for instead of my bunk. I was just dropping off with my head on one of the tables when the bosun came in and enquired if I thought the recreation room was a dosshouse. He told me I must get into my bunk if I wanted to sleep, and he didn't want to catch me dossing there again. I told him I found it difficult to sleep in my bunk with all the noise going on. His reply was one I had heard before.

Another sleepless night awaited me as the infernal din continued and I was driven to distraction by the fact nobody else seemed affected by it in the slightest. As soon as Fred climbed into his bunk he was fast asleep. Well, maybe I *did* catch an hour's sleep during the night – probably through sheer exhaustion – but I felt just as bad the following morning when I scrambled out of my bunk at first light and saw Fred – still fast asleep. I made my way amidships and snatched another half an hour with my head on one of the mess room tables.

The ship changed course and headed west. Bill Houston was one of the older hands and the one who always gave me good advice when needed. I asked him when I could learn to steer the ship to which he replied, the ship was at present in the Pentland Firth, where there was a lot of shipping around and the mate was unlikey to allow steering practice. However, because he was on the four to eight watch, he'd speak to Mr. Kirby and obtain permission for me at a later date. He pointed to the wake following the ship, telling me the idea was to keep it nice and straight or the officer on watch would see it and soon tell me off.

That night I felt I slept a bit better – maybe I *was* getting used to the noise.

The next day, we were clear of the Scottish coast and out into the Atlantic. Bill told me he'd spoken to the first mate, who'd given permission for me to go on the wheel with him at 19h00 for half an hour; he also said I must be neatly dressed. I was most excited and told all the people in the mess about my imminent steering lessons. All the greasers were having a go at me, and one of them suggested I'd have to wear a collar and tie with my best suit on when I went on the captain's bridge. Old George said he'd be off watch and didn't want to be woken up by the steering gear and all the extra racket I'd make. Another was implying that I'd sink the ship and said he'd be sitting by the boat deck with his lifejacket on. Anyway, 19h00 came and I was dressed nice and clean in an open-necked shirt with the trousers to my suit on, as my dungarees had holes in the knees with scrubbing out.

When I went up to the bridge, there was somebody on the starboard wing looking ahead over the dodger. As I arrived at the top of the ladder he turned around and I got a bit of a shock noticing the four gold bands on his sleeves which signified he was the captain. I was further surprised to see he was the bespectacled man I'd seen standing next to the Shipping Master in the South Shields shipping office. It was Captain Grist. I didn't know whether to speak, or what to say, or whether I should wait until spoken to. Eventually the captain spoke in a friendly manner, "Hello son, have you come to steer the ship?"

"Yes Sir," I replied with a stammer.

"Well," said the captain, "go and report to the mate, and keep a nice straight course." I reported to the mate asking him if I would be allowed to learn to steer the ship. He agreed and directed me over to where Bill Houston was standing on a grating, holding the wheel and peering into the compass binnacle.

I soon found out steering by a magnetic compass wasn't easy, as the compass card seemed to slither as though it was on an oil pad. Bill said in order to assist in the steering – while watching the compass card – I must also keep an eye on the ship's head, because even in the dark the ship's head can be seen to swing. While I was on the wheel with Bill, things seemed leisurely on the bridge, Captain Grist would walk from one wing of the bridge through the wheel house to the other side, his hands behind his back and in deep thought. The mate would sometimes be in the chart room, and sometimes he'd go out on the bridge wing and talk to the captain.

Half an hour went by, and although I was quite prepared to stay longer, the mate told me half an hour on the wheel was enough for the first day. Bill said something to me about the course but I misheard and went to walk out through the wheel house door. I was called back by Mr. Kirby who informed me whenever I left the wheel, I must always give the course I'd been steering to the mate on watch.

I had a look at the wake as I left the wheel house, it wasn't very long as the ship had only done about eleven knots, but at least it was straight. When I got down to the recreation room, the crowd was playing crib. As soon as I entered the room I was told the steering had been terrible, and although the midship section may have been OK, the after end of ship had rolled terribly and the quadrant had woken up all the men who were off watch.

I slept pretty well that night, and was able to get more work done the next day. I really believed I had a lot of work piled on me, especially in comparison with the cabin boys. Imagine my annoyance when I found out the two cabin boys were allowed overtime every day, as well as having every afternoon off from 13h00 until 15h00. I told the bosun about this and he agreed they were overpaid and underworked. I smiled thinking I was receiving sympathy until he told me that for the amount of work I completed, I was also overpaid.

The following night I had another good sleep and felt even more refreshed as I went up on deck to take the morning air. The air at sea really is something. It is so crisp, clean and healthy it makes me think how lucky seamen are to get away from all the smoke, coal dust, factories, and car fumes. The weather at sea has no equal with its blue skies, choppy seas, and a lovely fresh breeze from ahead, and of course the sight of the seagulls as they wheel around. Every time I emptied the gash bucket I would stand aft watching the wake of the ship.

The sailors had been telling me seagulls always follow ships. Not one seagull or two; not fifty or sixty – but for some strange reason always about fifteen to twenty for each ship, unless of course it's a fishing boat. Bill Houston told me all seagulls were reincarnated sailors and a captain always came back as an albatross. John Coyne, who was Bill's cabin and watch mate, intervened saying chief stewards always came back as jackdaws or buzzards. In the evening watch I spent another half an hour on the wheel with John Coyne, but it still wasn't easy.

The next morning at breakfast, the bosun told me Captain Grist would be doing rounds at 11h00. This meant I must really get stuck into my allotted tasks and have the accommodation gleaming on his arrival. Imagine my surprise when Paddy Fahy and Jock Niven from the eight to twelve watch began scrubbing out the mess room and pantry. I was sent aft to do the accommodation where I'd been told to bring the brass work right up to standard. There was no smoko during the morning, and at 10h55 after I'd finished my work aft, I made my way amidships to the mess room. Thanks to the eight to twelve watch, the place was absolutely sparkling and I thought it was cleaner than I could ever have made it. Meanwhile the crowd were aft, and would have to stand by their bunks or disappear as the captain made his inspection of the accommodation. I thought captain's rounds were supposed to be on a Sunday and couldn't understand why he was having them on a Tuesday.

The rounds party then arrived dressed in their uniforms. The first mate was at the head of the party, followed by the captain, the chief engineer, second engineer and chief steward – the bosun following up without uniform but looking very smart. I had a pleasant surprise when I saw the chief steward – the only other time I'd seen him was at the serving hatch when he gave the bond out. Now, having a good look, I realised I was just as tall as him. So at least I wasn't the shortest on the ship even if I was the skinniest.

The captain had a good look around the pantry, opened a drawer or two, peered inside the plate rack as well as the hot press and looked quite pleased.

Then he said, "You keep your mess room nice and clean, Peggy." I was just about to open my mouth and tell him the watch on deck were responsible for today's cleanliness when I saw the bosun put up his hand, indicating that I should remain silent. The captain then said to me, "I suppose you know what special day it is today don't you?" I stopped and thought before replying, "Rounds day sir?" The rounds party seemed quite amused by this, the captain then said with a smile on his face, "Peggy, today is June 2 and it's Coronation Day." I was astounded. I'd forgotten all about it; probably due to the excitement of the past week.

After the party left to inspect the rest of the 'midship accommodation, it was quiet and I supposed as soon as the inspection was completed, the crowd would return to the mess for smoko. A little while later when captains' rounds were over, I saw the party go up the starboard deck alleyway and back towards the bridge. By then I'd made the coffee and took it off the galley range awaiting the crowd's arrival. After about ten minutes nobody showed up, so I thought I'd better tell them the coffee was ready and went down aft. When I entered the recreation room, you could have knocked me down with a feather – just about all the sailors, greasers and stewards were in there, the tables full of beer, and everyone was in high spirits. Then I heard a familiar voice, "Come in scouse! Come and sit next to me and have a beer." I was doubly astonished – it was the bosun.

He had a huge grin on his face because in my absence, he'd relayed to everyone I didn't know it was Coronation Day. I sat down next to my tormentor and was asked if I'd ever had a beer before and would I like to have one. After replying I'd never drank alcohol in my life, the bosun put a bottle in front of me and even poured it out, telling me the captain had given everybody on the ship two beers, excepting the two cabin boys and myself because we were under eighteen. With the exception of those on essential duty, everyone had been give the day off and my gift from the captain was two bottles of lemonade.

The drinking and talking between the crowd was accompanied by a game of crib. I'd watched them playing this game before, and was fascinated as to how they could work out in a split second the many permutations of fifteen which could be obtained from the five cards. The bosun then suggested to everyone in the recreation room, if they agreed to do their own peggying, then I could have the rest of the day off. They all agreed as one and I finished my beer off pretending to like it. Unfortunately Jock Niven took this as a sign I would like another and after pouring it, told me to drink up. In a while I began to feel dizzy and went out on the after end for some fresh air. I noticed the seabirds which followed the ship and when they saw me they began squawking thinking they were about to be fed. Standing right aft I watched the wake being churned up by the propeller and a few minutes later felt a bit better. I then realised the ship had been at sea for a week, we were in mid-Atlantic, and the ship hadn't rolled one single bit. After the two bottles of beer I felt quite unsteady, maybe I was drunk.

On entering the recreation room again, I heard some of the greasers and sailors engaged in a heated discussion but when they saw me the dispute stopped. One of them suggested my opinion should be sought to settle the argument and I felt quite important. It was Old Bill Orbell who stood up, and whilst addressing me, pointed to George Chafer, another greaser, angrily saying George had claimed to have seen a one-man-band playing outside a Newcastle cinema. That this one-man-band had played a drum, a mouth organ, cymbals, a flute and other musical instruments all at the same time. "So what?" I slurred. "I saw one last week in South Shields, and I've seen lots of them in Liverpool." The recreation room went silent for a moment before howls of laughter showed their disbelief, but George Chafer came over to where I was sitting and patted me on the back, thanked me for my support on his side of the argument and gave me a beer. Although I didn't actually want the beer, I could hardly refuse as he was already pouring it, however with a small addition of lemonade, it tasted slightly better. I was quite delighted to think I'd settled the argument but Old Bill got up to question me again. He said as far as he was concerned, it was totally impossible for any man on earth to play two instruments at once, let alone half a dozen. Half way through my third beer, I was encouraged by the majority in the room to give a demonstration of just how this feat of musical artistry could ever be accomplished. Still sitting down, I mimicked the antics of the one-man-band which I'd seen so many times before.

By now the recreation room was full and there were those who said they couldn't see the performance, I was asked to stand up on the table so everybody could see properly. The bosun showed his delight at my agreement by granting me permission to climb on the table top. I soon realised I was rather drunk as my feet kept slipping off the table and several times I was saved from falling completely by outstretched hands. From what I can remember, I eventually sat down to some more beer not having the slightest idea what time it was, although, at some stage I was made to perform another demonstration for the man who had just come off the wheel – so it must have been either 14h00, 16h00, or even 18h00. The last thing I can recall about Coronation Day, was lying slumped unable to move on the settee in the recreation room.

Heavy Weather

I awoke shivering, my head was going round and round, and I tried to recollect my actions of the previous night. It then dawned on me I was suffering from one of the hangovers I'd heard people talking so much about; I felt so ill I just wanted to die. As my head continued to revolve I decided never to smoke or drink beer again. It then dawned on me, as a big sea smashed against the porthole, it wasn't just my head doing circles, but the ship was rolling – and heavily! It was barely daylight as I staggered from of my bunk, where I must have lain fully dressed and uncovered throughout the night. It was cold. I put more clothing on before going up on deck to see what was making the ship roll so much. The bosun was on the afterdeck with Fred and the farmer from the four to eight watch. They had oilskins and sea boots on and were putting up a lifeline from aft to the mast house, another from there to amidships was already up. They were using a Handy Billy to get the lifeline tight then making it fast to an eyeplate on the after bulkhead. When the bosun saw me, he said I must go to the mess room and make sure everything was secure as we were in for some heavy weather. The rolling of the ship didn't help my self-inflicted condition and I wondered if it was the effects of seasickness or the result of the beer and cigarettes.

The mess room was in a shambles as the ship pitched and rolled. Seats were piled up on each other, table condiments, ash trays and anything else that had been left loose slid freely around the deck. Each of the dining table seats had a chain from its base for screwing into the deck for when the ship rolled; but I'd never bothered securing the seats in order to save time whilst scrubbing out each morning. During each forenoon watch when I was at my busiest, the screwing on and off of these seats would have taken valuable time – besides, I never expected the ship to roll. I'd always thought it was too big. After a while when I'd ensured all was secure in the mess and pantry, I felt better as my head began to clear. I couldn't get over the fact just twelve hours earlier the ship had been sailing nicely along with a blue sea and sky, and not the slightest inclination of any change in the weather. But now the skies were dark and the sea quite rough.

A strong wind with big seas was coming from the port bow, and as I'd never seen or even imagined anything like it I wanted to see it all in detail. I climbed up the ladder to the boat deck and stood directly over the galley, from there I could see both sides of the ship and get a better view of the huge waves. What had yesterday been choppy blue water, was now big grey seas which came right up to the ship's side before breaking into a spray. I'd only been on the boat deck a couple of minutes when the bosun and Fred came along, I thought they were going to put a life line from the bridge to the galley but never found out. The bosun must have had the shock of his life when he saw me on the boat deck. "What the hell are you doing up there?" he screamed. "Are you bloody mad, get down off there and get below!" Well, I thought to myself, it was 05h00 and as I had to get my first ticking-off sometime, why not make an early start?

The ship continued to pitch and roll, the wind screamed overhead and occasionally when a real big one hit us it almost felt as though we'd collided with a mountain and the whole ship shuddered from stem to stern. Still clad in his heavy weather gear the bosun came into the mess room and cast a glaring look in my direction. He told me never again did he want to see me on deck in such conditions, because he didn't want to be the one who had to write a letter to my mother saying I'd disappeared at sea.

At seven bells, I was going aft to put the eight to twelve watch on the shake when suddenly the ship went quiet and the vibrating stopped. It didn't take much thought to realise the engines had stopped. After I'd woken the watch up, I saw all the engineers making their way down below into the engine room. George Chell was pulling two black balls up, which signified the engines had broken down and the ship was not under command.

The ship in its helpless state veered around, the sea and wind came from the port beam and the *Willesden* rolled wildly and violently. The wind screamed through the rigging as well as the topping lifts. The groaning of the ship as she hogged and sagged sounded like a herd of cattle being slaughtered. While the ship had been progressing under power, although rolling quite a bit, the galley was under control but now it was in a terrible state. The ship had rolled wickedly and the cook lost everything on

Above: The SS *Adviser* was owned by T&J Harrisons Lines of Liverpool. In 1952 she was being converted from coal to oil at Blyth.

Below: The SS *Clan Macnair*, broken up at Blyth in 1952

The 7043 ton MV *Willesden* was an Empire Boat built in 1944 as the *Empire Canning*.
She was taken over in 1946 by Watts Watts & Co. also known as the Britain Steamship Co.

Left: Painting on a stage

Above: An 'A' class Blue Funnel ship was in convoy with us through the Suez Canal.

Above: A Ship of the Strick Line, a common sight in the Suez Canal

Below: Brocklebank's four masted barque *Sindia* from an original oil painting by the author

Above: The MV *Georgic*, a bomb exploded inside her forward funnel during WW2.
The funnel was never replaced.

Below: The *Brittanic* was *Georgic*'s sister ship.

The 'Twickenham Twins' – Fred Hodges (on the left) and Sam Barter the Bosun

Above: The Eagle Oil tanker *San Velino*, could have been my first ship.

Below: The SS *Consuelo*, an Ellerman Wilson ship, was in Montreal with us.

The *Empress of Scotland* leaving Liverpool in the early 1950s. From an original oil painting by the author

the galley range before he had a chance to get the fire bars on. Eggs, bacon, beans, porridge and kits were all over the galley decks – fortunately nobody had been scalded.

Due to the violent movement of the ship, the creaking and groaning of the steel plates and its frames was quite something to listen to. It sounded as though the whole ship needed oiling. I can never remember which fool told me big ships don't roll, nor who told me when a ship rolls more than thirty-three degrees, it passes the mark of its stability and keeps on going over. I decided I wouldn't bother listening to people any more – the ship I believed was too big to roll really did roll, and more than thirty-three degrees; I'm positve of that. At times the ship would buck and kick so much, if I wasn't careful I'd be thrown upwards to bang my head on the deckhead. I can now well imagine what a cowboy at a rodeo goes through when he's on a wild stallion.

It was not possible to scrub out that day. In fact it was hardly possible to do anything and it took a supreme effort just to keep one's feet. However, I did manage to get the coffee made, and as directed put wet tea towels on all the tables to stop the mugs rolling off. As I sat in the mess with the sailors, I found out why everyone was issued with a big pint mug for their tea or coffee. In the heavy weather the pint pots would be only half filled, then when the ship rolled one way or the other, the contents of the mug wouldn't spill out. It was during smoko when one of the greasers came in, saying an attempt was soon to be made to re-start the engines. Shortly after there was a bang of compressed air from the engine room, followed by the sound of the rickety engine coming back to life. However, the joy of being re-started was short lived for the engine died again.

Amidst the violent rolling of the ship the whole of the engine room crowd were down below, even Mr. Duncan the chief engineer was there with his white overalls on. Sometime later in the forenoon watch the engines were re-started. This re-start enabled the ship to get back on course, and the violent rolling decreased to mere heavy rolling, however, it wasn't long before the engines stopped again. The wind and sea came back with such a fury, once again the big combers broke over the port side and the ship bounced like a cork. I spent as much time as I could watching the seas smash right over the ship and wondered just what she looked like from a distance. It must have been a really spectacular sight with the spray reaching over the masts and focs'le head. One day, I thought, I would like to paint pictures like this. That is, if I ever got back to land.

The ship's cook was unable to prepare any kind of a meal that day and as the galley fire went out we had tinned beans, tea, bread and butter. It wasn't easy to make a pot of tea and I was relieved of this job in case I slid over in the mess room and scalded myself. Sleeping in a bunk was difficult too so bunk boards were fitted to save everyone from being thrown out of their nest.

One thing I did learn all to quickly was when I went to the toilet, I had to make the visit as short as possible. It so happened that when sitting on 'the throne' during heavy rolling, the seawater often rushed up the scupper pipes with some force and gave my bum a good soaking. The water could be heard coming up with a rushing gurgling noise and it seemed only the inexperienced were caught with their pants down. There was a handrail on the bulkhead to hang on to during heavy rolling, the sailors called them straining bars.

Because of the heavy weather the bosun advised me I must only go from amidships to aft when absolutely necessary in case I got washed over the wall. This advice went unheeded – in fact I was enjoying the heavy weather so much, I made as many trips from amidships to aft and back as possible. One of the main reasons for my new found enjoyment, was the rolling was too bad to permit the scrubbing out of the mess room and the rest of the accommodation. The only drawback was the lack of watertight doors on the after accommodation meant this became flooded after a big Green 'un swept right down the companionway. This resulted in a couple of feet of water in the forward cabins. Now I fully realised why Fred had chosen the after cabin – our cabin was at the after end of the sheer and was two or three feet higher than the forward cabins, and dry. All hands were now engaged in baling out using their dhobi buckets in a chain gang. I was left to finally make the alleyways dry. An hour or so later just as I'd finished the drying out, another sea came down the companionway and once again it was the forrard cabins which became flooded – we had to start all over again.

The engines started and broke down several times. Two red 'not under command lights' were hoisted during the hours of darkness, this signal was to replace the black balls of the daylight hours and the merry song and dance of pitching and rolling continued all through the night.

During the next morning with the ship's engines still idle, and with no change in the weather or the violent rolling, I was in for a bit of a shock. Attempting to make the trip from aft to amidships, there were three greasers huddled in a group standing and waiting on the starboard side by the poop housing. The seas were sweeping over and across the hatches while they waited for a chance between the seas to make the dash amidships. They were all rather cautious being older men, but when I saw them huddled up in their little group I began to laugh at them. By now I was aware I'd been cleverly set up to do the one-man-band show and was looking for revenge. Being nimble and fleet of foot and wearing a pair of baseball boots, I gave the old men a demonstration of running from aft to amidships, then back again to show them how easy it was to make the transit. The seas were still sweeping over and they continued to wait their chance. The shock came the next time I was halfway through my performance and reached as far as the forward end of number six hatch. Suddenly I slipped on the recently painted deck and slithered right out to the ship's side as she rolled over to starboard, realising with horror that I was in 'no mans land'. The ship, which was rolling more than thirty-degrees each way then began her roll back to port. As I lay spread-eagled on the deck I saw one of the huge greeny grey seas looming over from the port side. I scrambled across the slippery deck and crawled as fast as I could to the lee of hatch coaming. From there I grabbed at anything at all to hang on to; finding a ring bolt which I grasped with both hands I clung to for dear life. As the sea swept right over the hatch and me I could feel its power trying to tear me away from the ring bolt, but somehow or other I held on.

Visibly shocked I got up and joined the waiting group, as the ship seemed to steady for a moment, and one of the greasers shouted, "Now." We all made the dash for the sanctuary of the mast house between number five and six hatches. From there we had a further wait for the next short lull in the weather. Shaken up a bit, or I should say a lot, I went with them and reached the mess room feeling rather sheepish. Once inside, Old George growled, "Ye bloody young upstart – that'll larn ye." They all had a good laugh at my expense. The bosun wasn't around, and he never did find out about the incident. The greasers knew I'd learned my lesson and there was no need for them to tell. For my part, it didn't take much to realise, if the ringbolt I'd caught hold of wasn't in its exact place as I grabbed out for anything at all to hold onto, I'd have either been smashed up against the guardrails, gone over the wall, or probably both. During the rest of my six-month stay on the *Willesden*, and unbeknown to anybody else, whenever I passed the forward end of number six hatch, I often said a little thank you to the ringbolt.

As far as the weather was concerned the next day was just as bad; big seas, heavy rolling, and low flying black nimbus clouds racing past. The hurricane must have been at least force twelve but I never found out. The sea and the sky seemed almost black with no break in the blanket of dark grey cloud cover. I liked watching some of the huge seas come over, noting how they'd break into combers then smash against the ship. Sometimes one would flash with a brilliant opalescent green making me wonder from where the light could come to form such a beautiful colour.

During the lunch hour I was standing right aft watching this great feat of nature, marvelling how when the ship pitched forward the stern and the propeller would lift right up out of the water. Then as the ship pitched aft, the sea would come right up to the deck, it felt like being on a giant see-saw. Suddenly from behind me there was a scream louder than the hurricane – it was the bosun in his oilskins. Ranting and raving he told me to get in off the deck before the ship was pooped. When he got me into the accommodation his face was livid and his eyes blazing. He told me if I were to be seen going over the side, a boat would have to be launched with seven men in it; their lives would be in mortal danger, and all because I couldn't do as I was told. The air was absolutely blue and I was informed if there was any more of it, I should have my bags packed and ready by the time we reached Montreal.

I hadn't realised if anyone were seen going over the side, a lifeboat would be launched to save him. This would of course put the crew of the lifeboat in real danger. I never went wave watching again.

The heavy weather and the breakdowns continued. I counted fourteen engine failures over the three days and maybe there were more while I slept. However, the problem, whatever it was, was eventually discovered and rectified. One of the greasers later told me it was a fault which should have been detected to during the ship's long stay in South Shields.

Next day the weather improved greatly, what had also improved was my sleeping. By now I was reasonably used to the propeller, the creaking and groaning of the frames and the ship's vibrations, I never seemed to bang my head on doorways anymore either.

I went on the wheel again for the next two nights and thought at last I was getting the hang of steering the ship. The bosun said I'd better be good on the wheel by the end of the trip, and if I were, despite my stupid behaviour at times, he'd consider letting me come back on the next voyage to wherever it may be.

That day the sun came out, white cumulus clouds filled the sky and the sea was blue again. I was rather surprised when I went down aft to empty the gash bucket to see the seagulls again. During the last few days when we'd been in heavy weather I hadn't seen any seagulls and had thought the ones which had started the trip with us had all gone back home. Now the weather was good again they'd returned, and they were the same ones too. One or two I could recognise, and as I stood there waiting to empty the bucket, I wondered where they'd been while the heavy weather was in progress. One in particular, which I could identify out of all the others, used to make a lot of squawking and seemed to be the senior of them all. I called him Sam after the bosun because he made the most noise. He spent much of his time perched on the truck of the signal mast and each time he arrived there he would make a loud squawk, chasing the other birds away.

As I put the bucket up on the rail, this hard-faced seagull came right up to me and started squealing and squawking as though telling me to hurry up. "Shut up Sam, you Bristol bastard!" I shouted as it went gliding past in the wind. "Wait your turn like all the others." Just then I heard a sniggering behind me. It was Mr. Perkins the chief steward. "Oh, just wait till I tell the bosun what I heard you say," he said in his machine gun cockney accent. Then he added, "I'm also going to tell the second cook on you, for giving his bread to the birds." I was shocked out of my skin. "I didn't mean the bosun," I said to the chief. "I meant someone else." But the chief steward was unconvinced, "Oh well," he said, " if it was only someone else you were calling a 'Bristol bastard', then you won't mind me telling the bosun." Mr. Perkins then turned his little fat body around and went amidships giggling and sniggering. When I'd later plucked up enough courage to enter the mess room, the bosun was in there, but except for giving me a little glare he didn't say anything. I went into the galley for the soup and the second cook didn't say anything either. Maybe the chief steward had second thoughts, and if I kept out of his way he might forget the incident altogether. At 18h00 there was a bond issue. I didn't go in case I jogged the chief steward's memory. This meant I had to sacrifice two hundred cigarettes for calling a seagull names.

On Monday June 8, I was in the mess room scrubbing out when suddenly a shout came through the porthole from the bosun, "Hey scouse, come out here and have a look at this." From my place of worship on my hands and knees I went out on the deck. The bosun pointed over the starboard side where there was an iceberg some way off. He explained what could be seen of the iceberg was less than a quarter of its mass, and there was a lot more of it under water. He asked me if I'd ever seen an iceberg before and of course I said I hadn't. He had a wicked glint in his eyes as he told me the first one he'd ever seen was in the River Mersey because it's always so cold there. The bosun could see the look of bewilderment on my face and roared with laughter before ordering me back to my hands and knees job. I saw a few more icebergs during the morning, but in the windless grey afternoon it became quite cold and a thick fog descended. The ship slowed down, and the steam whistle was sounded every two minutes as we crawled along at four or five knots. Suddenly I heard a whistle from another ship, eerily sounding more like a dog yowling. Sometimes the sound appeared to be coming from ahead, then it was on the beam and then from astern – it was like a ventriloquist ship. Old Fred said it wasn't a ship's whistle that could be heard at all, it was one of those wind-up foghorns, probably from a fishing boat. The fog thickened until it was like the proverbial pea-souper with visibility down to just a few yards. The *Willesden*, which was without radar, stopped its engines. Someone remarked it was a pity the *Titanic* hadn't done the same thing when she was in the same area just over forty years previously. The fog lifted and returned a few times and in concert the ship intermittently stopped and started its engines. When we were making way the whistle was sounded every two minutes, but when the engines were stopped it was once a minute.

At smoko time, I went up to the wheelhouse with a cup of coffee for the helmsman. The captain was on the bridge and looking most concerned. As usual I hung about taking stock of all the procedures. Every two minutes, the third mate would go out on the bridge wing and pull the whistle lanyard. This was connected to the brass steam whistle on the forward side of the funnel. The result was a burst of steam and a deep muffled roar from the ship's whistle. Since the first time I'd heard the ship's whistle and seen how it was done, I'd always wanted to operate the lanyard. I asked Mr. Collister if I could possibly do this, and even offered to relieve him while he attended to more important tasks. He said I couldn't and sent me off the bridge. Due to the foggy weather conditions, I was not allowed on the wheel for the rest of the passage. Ed Merson came down from the bridge and told us about an iceberg we had nearly hit. He said he was bang on course with visibility just a couple of ship lengths and the ship making about four knots; suddenly the fog lifted to reveal an iceberg a mile away and right ahead.

The crowd were soojying the white paintwork in the deck alleyway outside the mess and it was pretty cold. They remarked how lucky I was to be the peggy, with such a nice warm job, I replied saying I didn't like the job and would gladly swap with them if I could.

By June 10 with the weather crisp and clear we were in the Straights of Belle Isle. From there land could be seen from both sides of the ship, however the sighting soon diminished again and it appeared we were once more out in the open sea. Because of the long run up the river there were now two pilots on board, each to relieve the other as needed. They would be taking us up as far as Quebec where they would change with another pilot who would complete the passage to Montreal.

The land appeared again. The ship was now in the St. Lawrence River where the weather became warmer. Once again the bosun called me out on deck from my position of scrubbing out in the mess room. He showed me an 'Empress Boat' going down the starboard side, explaining the ship – which was the three funneled passenger liner *Empress Of Scotland* – was on its way to Liverpool where it would arrive in four or five days time. He told me the ships of the Canadian Pacific Railways ran a three week round trip from Liverpool to Montreal, but they didn't have a good name and were referred to as hungry.

I had a habit of talking to anyone who I thought could offer me information concerning the *Willesden's* progress. George Chell was always an easy target; he knew a lot of what was happening due to his position as an apprentice; he listened to a lot of the gossip in the saloon. However, and although it was no secret, he told me it would take another two days to make Montreal as we were pushing against a fast flowing current.

Soon we were at Quebec and the pilots changed over while the ship was still making way. I saw the Chateau Frontenac and the cliffs which must have been four hundred feet high. These were the cliffs I'd been taught about at school, the ones General Wolff and his army had scaled.

Before I joined the ship I'd somehow thought there would be seamanship lessons on board ship for the likes of me, there was no such thing. Instead, I had to watch, listen, ask, and be careful – for example as the derricks were being topped, I noticed some of them had single span topping lifts with big chains and a monkey plate, whilst others were rove through the derrick head blocks. There was no apparent reason for this mixing of the topping lifts and nobody seemed to know, except the ship had been built during the war where anything and everything was thrown in for general use. I was on the guys when the derricks went up and watched a chain stopper getting used, later on with Bill Houston helping me as I practiced it a few times.

Montreal

We arrived at Montreal on the evening of June 13, having been at sea for seventeen days. Five or six days had been lost due to bad weather, break downs, fog, and sailing against the current of the St. Lawrence River. When we tied up I was on the focs'le along with Mr. Kirby the mate, the bosun, four sailors and Achmid the chippy who drove the windlass. The bosun let me put the rope stopper on one of the headlines watching me carefully as I did so; I'd practiced this in the sea school but to do it in a real situation was quite pleasing and I felt chuffed. After doing the head ropes we done the forrard headspring where a chain stopper was used to hold the weight before putting the wires on the bitts.

No sooner had we tied up than the hatches were stripped and the hatch boards stacked up on the deck – the beams were left on. I was surprised to find there were three tarpaulins to each hatch and on making inquiries, was told without three tarps, and considering the weather we'd been through, the *Willesden* would probably be at the bottom of the Atlantic. I collected all the wedges in a sack and took them up to the chippy's shop under the focs'le head.

A load of timber was lowered down into each hold, it was made up of big thick planks which were to be used in making the shifting boards and would help prevent the grain cargo from moving. A gang of shore chippies, along with Achmid, went down into the holds and began erecting the shifting boards. They would work throughout the night. Ahead of us was a ship, with a green hull, red funnel and a black top. She was the *Consuelo* of Hull and belonged to Ellerman Wilson Lines. I thought at first she was a much smaller ship than the *Willesden*. This was because she was almost fully laden, whereas our ship having had the deep tanks pumped out towered above her. Paddy Fahy informed me, however, that both vessels were Empire Boats of 7,000 tons and were virtual sister ships. The words of Worms Worthington who was now on the *San Velino* came back to me, "Empire Boats – you'll see them in every port you go." In the opposite berth, there was a ship called the *Roonagh Head.* She had a red hand on her black funnel and was registered at Belfast. Ahead of her was a French ship that someone said was a converted T2 Tanker also awaiting a grain cargo.

Despite the fact I still had the 36/- from my advance note, I'd put my name down for a £2 sub. It was the chief steward who allocated the sub, but when he cast his crafty little eyes on me he wanted to know why I wanted the money. I told him I was going to buy books on how to draw ships. The rest of the crowd had gone to the local pubs called Joe Beefs or the Liverpool Arms; I'd been invited to go along but after the Coronation Day episode nobody was ever going to see me drink beer again. On Saturday afternoon I went ashore but was disappointed when I couldn't find any of the books I was looking for, although I did get lots of pencils, drawing paper, and erasers.

Later in the afternoon I went aboard the *Consuelo* where I met my opposite number, the peggy. He told me the whole crowd were from Hull, it was a good ship, and he was going back in her on the next trip. They were also going to Hull with their grain cargo and should arrive a few days ahead of the *Willesden.*

With the paper and pencils I'd purchased, I began trying to draw the scenes I'd witnessed in the Atlantic, with the ship pitching and rolling the way she had; my preliminary efforts were a disaster. I would begin by starting at the focs'le head, drawing in all its surroundings, then I'd do the fore deck, followed by the bridge, but on reaching the afterdeck and poop, I would run off the paper. Criticism and encouragement were lavishly showered on me by those who came to observe my attempts, however my mind was focused on the finished product, I knew it was going to take time to be able to draw ships, and one day I'd be successful. Old Bill Orbell who helped and encouraged me in my drawing said I should first mark out the stem and stern, followed by all the other important structures like the focs'le, bridge, 'midship accommodation and then the poop. It was more logical to do it this way – and it worked. Although it was still hard work, it was an enjoyable struggle.

The shore carpenters had finished erecting the shifting boards and we were awaiting the departure of the *Consuelo* so we could move into her berth. I watched her as she sailed, she was right down on her marks and I had a good idea of just what we would look like when we left. The only difference between the two vessels I could see, was the *Consuelo*, being a steamship, had a taller funnel and only five hatches compared to the *Willesden*'s six. No sooner had the *Consuelo* left than the *Willesden* was warped up the quayside to take her place at the grain shutes. This was done with the aid of the windlass and it wasn't long before the grain began rushing down the shutes and into the empty holds. At number two hold there was a mark on the inside of the hatch coaming to say that the ship was 4,043 tons net. Just above on the bridge was a brass plate stating the ship had been built by the Caledon ship building Co. in 1944 and was numbered 166219.

During our stay in Montreal I looked around the city as much as I could and the weather was lovely and warm, but I didn't care much about ever going back there. Many of the French speaking people were unfriendly and only spoke to me when I was buying something.

A few days later we were fully loaded and preparing to sail. While the hatches were being battened down I was given the job of helping Achmid to wedge up. He directed me to drag a sack of wedges around after him, placing them between the battens and the cleats. He would then follow up with his seven-pound hammer driving the wedges home, when occasionally I put a wedge in the wrong way he would correct me in a good natured manner. I liked the chippy a lot, he came from Estonia and the bosun was always ribbing him about being a gannet, but he always had a smile on his face and all the time I knew him I never once saw him annoyed.

Homeward Bound

On our way down the Saint Lawrence River and homeward bound for Hull, things were different. Instead of the ship labouring her way up stream against the current, she was really flying and George the apprentice told me the ship was doing fifteen knots. Added to which, as George McIntosh had assured me three weeks earlier, the propeller was now so far under the water it could hardly be heard. The vibrations had ceased with the 10,000 of cargo, although the quadrant still made its hissing, clackety noise. By now however, I was used to it. We passed a lot of shipping as we sped down the river and one that was pointed out to me was the single-funelled *Empress of Australia*, of the Canadian Pacific Railways. She had only been in service for that company for a few weeks, having replaced the *Empress Of Canada* which had burned out in Liverpool's Gladstone Dock five months earlier. The other vessel which completed the trio of ships on the Liverpool to Montreal run was the *Empress of France*.

Soon the ship was back out in the Atlantic with the weather clear. The bosun told me I had to go on the wheel at 09h45 under the guidance of the helmsman. The watches had changed at Montreal, and those who were in the four to eight watch on the outward passage, were now in the eight to twelve watch, so I spent ten minutes with John Coyne before steering unsupervised. John would leave the wheel and walk forward looking out of the wheel house window checking me now and again and it wasn't long before he gave the course to Mr. Collister the third mate and went down for his smoko. For the next half an hour I had no problems and was relieved by the ordinary seaman at 10h30. I gave the course to Mr. Collister before dashing out onto the bridge wing to see how straight the wake was.

The next morning when I went on the wheel the ordinary seaman gave me the course saying the ship had a following sea and was steering 'like a bastard'. I wasn't sure what this meant but I soon found out. Although the weather was good it was extremely difficult to keep the course, and on a couple of occasions I was ten degrees off. Each time the third mate went past the wheel, he would look at the compass to check the course, and each time he did so I was either on or close to the course. Mr. Collister then went into the chartroom saying if I saw any ships I must alert him. I was struggling with the wheel and thought how glad I'd be when I was relieved. Then I heard a voice from the bridge wing, "Hey there, we're going to Hull not Liverpool." I froze! It was the captain. He told me to come out on the bridge wing and have a look at the wake. I looked at the wheel, and then at him, as if to imply that the wheel couldn't be left unattended. The captain assured me the ship would steer better without my steering skills and not to worry. I left the wheel and went out on the bridge wing. The captain pointed astern at the wake and told me it looked like a dog's hind leg – I was using too much wheel and mustn't chase the compass. He informed me we were liable to run out of coal long before we arrived at our destination if everyone steered the ship like me. I couldn't help wondering why he said we'd run out of coal. I was glad when my half an hour was up, although I did learn something new that day and that was about a following sea. When I got back down below I told Jock Niven of my steering and the captain saying we would run out of coal, but Jock just laughed and said the Old Man must have thought he was still in one of the coal burners he'd previously been on. I didn't go on the wheel the next morning as the weather came up again, it didn't seem as bad as the outward passage, but then we were in ballast and now we were loaded deep. Maybe the weather on the outward passage looked worse than it actually was because of the ship breaking down – I was unable to make any kind of comparison.

When the seas began rising again, I went down to the cabin to ensure the portholes were battened down. On arrival I saw although the portholes appeared secure, there was water leaking through and into the drip tray beneath. I decided they needed further tightening and produced my, as yet, unused marlin-spike from the drawer and was about to begin when Fred arrived on the scene. He told me to put the spike away and tightened the butterfly clips by hand, advising me that portholes should be tightened by hand only; the pressure applied by a marlin-spike would crack the glass and might even blow the glass out.

The weather stayed heavy for a further two days, with the ship behaving well even though I thought the wind was probably force ten. It seemed to me there was less water coming over the decks than there was outward bound, probably because the ship's engines were not breaking down. I only managed one more half an hour on the wheel, as we were now approaching the Scottish coast.

Something else I noticed on this homeward run was we hadn't seen a single iceberg. It made me wonder if Captain Grist had taken the ship south of Newfoundland to avoid the icebergs and the fog, for some reason I never asked.

One evening after tea, I was clearing up while the sailors were having a discussion in the mess. They were talking about some of the ships they'd sailed on and, as usual, I was keenly interested in what they had to say. I listened to John Coyne describing his last ship *The Lady Charrington.* He gave a glowing account of the vessel with its abundant overtime and excellent conditions, comparing it most favourably to the *Willesden.* Then I put my foot in it asking him if it was such a good ship why had he left it. I didn't mean to upset him but I certainly did, and while everyone was having a laugh at him, he jumped up screaming I should be seen and not heard. One of the sailors winked at me as I suffered this outburst, later telling me *The Lady Charrington* was nothing more than a collier on North-east Articles. Conditions on all these colliers were bad and they were good ships to keep clear of. He told me these colliers signed a North-east Agreement which was different than the one we were presently on, and everyone had to pay as much as 25/- a week for their food – the colliers were 'cold, wet, floating fleabags'.

Fortunately, John Coyne did not hold grudges because during the next morning at smoko, both him and Bill Houston asked me what my plans were when the ship paid off. I shrugged and said I'd try and get another ship. They both told me I should make another trip in the *Willesden*, the shipping master wouldn't like it if he seen one five-week engagement for a first tripper in my discharge book. I explained to them the bosun had promised me a free railway warrant, meaning I would be sacked. Paddy Fahy then chippped in saying he hoped he was due for a free railway ticket because he certainly didn't want to come back for another trip. The bosun, who was listening to all this from the pantry, then shouted Paddy mustn't worry, his railway warrant had already been arranged.

§

At lunchtime we were all sitting in the mess when the bosun bounced in. He'd just come from a meeting with the first mate and was in a particularly good mood. He was singing one of his rather humorous little songs, about the prince and princess of fairyland who were engaged in a new position of love making (this cannot be written or repeated).

After he'd finished singing his solo masterpiece which he'd no doubt composed himself, he made an announcement for all to hear.

The news he'd just received from Mr. Kirby, was after the ship had discharged at Hull, she was to load a general cargo at Newcastle and London then proceed to India. The bosun's speech was greeted with groans of disappointment from a those who must have been planning another trip on the ship. The bosun then went on to say clothing in India was cheap, and while the ship was there maybe the peggy would be able to buy a new pair of dungarees. The message by the bosun implied I was free to make another voyage in the *Willesden*. "Are you coming back scouse?" the bosun asked with a grin on his face, I nodded quite happily, but then he told me I could only come back, if I did the one man band demonstration for him. Everyone had a laugh, but I told the bosun when I'd done the show on Coronation Day I was drunk, and if he wanted me to do it again he'd have to buy me four beers to get me drunk again. Those in the mess had another laugh but it was on the bosun this time. Later on, I spoke to the bosun and told him although I liked the ship, I didn't like the peggy's job. He replied saying a new deck boy was to be signed on at Hull, he would be the new peggy and now I could steer I would go into a watch.

It was June 27 and the weather was really warm as we sailed through the Pentland Firth at the north of Scotland. When I'd tried to release the porthole butterfly clips I found them too tight where Fred had screwed them up, I didn't try to loosen them with the spike in case I turned the wrong way and cracked the glass, but it was no problem for Fred when he arrived. By this time I'd used up all my paper and couldn't do any more drawing so I decided to prepare my go-ashore gear for paving off. I only had one go-ashore shirt and was ironing it in the recreation room; I thought I was pretty good at ironing but Paddy Fahy said I was doing it wrong. He then wet the shirt again, hung it out in the breeze for half an hour, then showed me the way he did his and I learned something new about ironing.

On Saturday afternoon, the sailors and greasers were all sitting on number six hatch and trying their best to rib me. Being a bit short of clothing, I was identified as being 'schooner rigged', and one of the greasers asked me if I wanted to buy a briefcase which he had for sale. When I asked him what good was a briefcase to me, he replied saying I could use it to put all my clothing in when I went on leave. That when I walked down the gangway with my briefcase, everyone would think I was the shipping master and raise their hats to me. Then they tried me on another saying I had the channels, and sure enough, and very soon after, one of the sailors came running excitedly down the deck. He said the ship was to return to Montreal, then after discharging the grain cargo she was to go on a two-year trip to Russia and hoped everyone had plenty of warm clothing. The audience gasped and looked at me to see my reaction, but I told them I didn't care, and asked them, if the ship was going back to Montreal, why hadn't she changed course. It went on all afternoon until Paddy Fahy said he'd show me the burning finger trick; Paddy's real name was John, he only got that name Paddy because he came from Galway. He was a very powerfully built man and extremely strong. To show me the trick, Paddy said I must go and ask the chippy for a six-inch nail. The chippy refused saying his shop was locked up and he didn't have one anyway, but the others said he was a company's man and too tight to oblige.

Paddy then went down to his cabin and came back with a six-inch nail and some old socks. He wrapped the socks around the ends of the nail, then began bending the nail back and forth until it snapped. He thengave me the two broken portions to examine, however on taking them from him, I jumped like a scalded cat as the broken nail portions were burning hot with friction. With a smile Paddy told me now I knew how to do the burning finger trick. Later on Paddy gave me another of his six-inch nails and asked me if I could break it, and if I could, he'd stick the ends in his mouth and burn it. He told me if he burned his mouth, he wouldn't be able to eat his meals and I could eat all his grub for the rest of the trip. I took the nail and wrapped it in the socks he'd supplied, but after a strenuous effort all I could achieve was one little bend in the nail.

During the night of June 29, I was asleep in my bunk as the ship progressed down the North Sea; the noise from the propeller deep under water was more a steady humming as it revolved at its ninety rpm. In comparison with the outward passage its noise didn't bother me at all, as neither did the hissing of steam and the clackety-clacking from the steering gear, nor indeed any of the general noises from down aft. I had by now and like everybody else, become accustomed to the movement and noises of the ship; but suddenly I was woken up by a strange new feeling. Silence! The ship had stopped. Soon after and through the open porthole I heard the anchor cable running out, we were at anchor in the River Humber, early next morning the sailors who'd been on anchor watch put the pilot ladder over and the mud pilot came aboard. Just before breakfast we entered the King George V Dock.

It was a great pity the trip had been so short, the crowd had hardly the chance to know each other before the ship paid off. The only members of the deck crowd to make a return voyage were the bosun, Fred Hodges, John Coyne, Bill Houston, and myself. I do know Paddy Fahy had his wish granted by getting a free railway warrant. That Ed Merson was going to sit his EDH examination, but the rest paid off because they didn't fancy the run to India. The leave system worked out I was entitled to eight days leave per year, or one day for each forty-five days service. For every Sunday the ship was at sea one additional day's leave is granted, or for half a Sunday – half a day's leave; there was also an extra day for the public holiday of Coronation Day, so for the short voyage, I had seven day's leave.

I scrubbed out the mess room and locking it up with a sigh of relief gave the key to the bosun; I hated the peggy's job and was glad a new deck boy was to sign on. The bosun then suggested to me, as he was living aboard during my seven days leave, I could keep my belongings in his cabin; this was to prevent any thieves who were sometimes seen wandering around paid off ships. As my suitcase had previously fell apart with the sea water, I later deposited a shopping bag in his cabin with all my gear in it. The poor bosun was speechless before he went into a fit of laughing at my lack of clothing, because all I had except the clothes I stood up in was the working clothes he'd seen me in every day. We paid off in the saloon, my wages for the trip was £7-11-8, but I also got a free 18/- third class return ticket from Hull to Liverpool. Although I still had the 36/- from my advance note, I couldn't help thinking about the 4/- commission I'd wasted in getting it. Nevertheless, I'd never been so rich or well fed, and so ended my first trip to sea.

Crew list of the MV *Willesden* which signed on at Hull
Wednesday July 8, 1953.

Name	Rank	Age	Address	MonthlyWage	Last Ship
FW Grist	Master	48	Berkshire	?	*Twickenham*
J Kirby	1st Mate	26	Newport	£52-10s	*Willesden*
O Brown	2nd Mate	28	Edinburgh	£42-10	*Willesden*
J Collister	3rd Mate	24	Hornchurch	£33-15	*Willesden*
J Egan	Radio Officer	27	Sunderland	£38-0	*Flowergate*
G Chell	Apprentice	19	Stroud	£8-00	*Willesden*
W Kerr	Apprentice	18	Belfast	£6-00	?
S Barter	Bosun	27	Bristol	£31-5	*Willesden*
A Wichmann	Carpenter	57	Estonia	£33-10	*Willesden*
H Wilson	AB	26	Hull	£28-0	*Cape Rodney*
G Smith	AB	25	Hull	£26-0	*Cape Rodney*
M Bayes	AB	24	Scarborough	£28-0	*Martland*
W Houston	AB	29	Hebburn on Tyne	£28-0	*Willesden*
J Coyne	AB	33	South Shields	£28-0	*Willesden*
F Hodges	AB	29	Portishead	£28-0	*Willesden*
T Megginson	SOS	19	Hull	£18-0	*Hudson Sound*
P Dolan	SOS	19	Hull	£18-0	*Memphis*
J Cunningham	Deck Boy	18	Bradford	£10-0	*Baron Haig*
J Dick	JOS	22	Hull	£15-10	*Baltavia*
J Richardson	Deck Boy	16	Liverpool	£10-0	*Willesden*
E Duncan	Ch. Engineer	59	West Lothian	£82-10	*Willesden*
W Atkinson	2nd Engineer	34	Walker on Tyne	£67-10	*Woodford*
J Murray	3rd Engineer	28	Greenock	£36-15	*Willesden*
M Lewis	4th Engineer	22	Glamorgan	£30-0	*Willesden*
W Gibson	Jnr Engineer	21	Glasgow	£28-0	*Willesden*
G Fagan	Jnr Engineer	23	Old Penshaw	£28-0	*Willesden*
R Collins	Jnr Engineer	21	Barry	£28-0	*Willesden*
G McIntosh	Greaser	46	Glasgow	£30-5	*Willesden*
W Orbell	Greaser	55	Kirby	£30-5	*Willesden*
A Leonard	Greaser	61	Durham	£30-5	*Willesden*
M Arney	Greaser	25	Hull	£30-5	*St. Elwyn*
J Chafer	Greaser	34	Barton on Humber	£30-5	*Willesden*
A Robins	Greaser	49	Durham	£30-5	*Baltavia*
J Perkins	Ch. Steward	52	Cardiff	£37-10	*Willesden*
J Hall	2nd Steward	31	Hull	£27-10	*British Commander*
J Dawson	Asst. Steward	26	South Shields	£27-0	*Cutturo*
R Gascoigne	Ship's Cook	25	Bridlington	£34-10	*Athenic*
P Kingham	2nd Cook	21	Hull	£28-10	*Indian City*
R Stafford	Pantry Boy	17	Hull	£10-0	*St. Elwyn*
J Levitt	Cabin Boy	17	Hull	£10-0	*Borodino*

Second Trip First Ship

At Hull, and on July 8 1953 I once again signed on the ship as a deck boy; the signing on ceremony took place in the saloon. The mess room I'd left so nice and clean was now full of dockers and hardly in the same condition I'd left it in. I wasn't really bothered though, because the new deck boy who was to join on the following day was to be the new peggy. The bosun told me he'd considered and understood the fact I didn't like being the peggy, and as he'd got a new deck boy for the ship, I should clean up all the accommodation in view of his arrival. This was no problem, and I was quite pleased to do it for what I thought would be the last time; but when the new heir apparent to the peggy's job arrived the next day, the bosun said he had some bad news for me. He informed me the new deck boy had just completed a nine month voyage and was due for promotion to JOS; I was to remain as peggy for the voyage.

Although I felt disappointed I knew it wasn't the bosun's fault; besides, and as he'd told me, if I had paid off and gone to another ship I'd still have been the peggy. However, the bosun went on to explain as well as the downturns there were also some advantages to be gained in the peggy's job. For example, if I were to make sandwiches for the dockers from the left over eggs and bacon, then make a brew of coffee for them, I could make quite a bit of extra money. This soon turned out to be a good sideline, and the new ship's cook Ron Gascoigne who'd learned of my new business venture, threw in quite a few extra eggs for breakfast. I made an extra £2 before leaving Hull during the week. Later on I saw pinned on the notice board the list of the outward bound ports we were to visit after London. On the outward passage our first stop was Genoa, then Port Said, Port Sudan, Aden,

Colombo, Madras, Vizagapatnam, Calcutta ending up at Chittagong. There was no list of the homeward ports, but it was expected the same ones would be visited when the ship was homeward bound. The ship being a tramp was on charter to the P&O Line. I heard the bosun saying the good thing about being on the charter, was as both companies had the same black funnel markings, there'd be no need to re-paint our funnel.

While on leave I'd bought some gear so I wouldn't be so schooner rigged as I'd been during the last trip. This included a suitcase, an oilskin, sou'wester, seaboots, these items had cost nearly £2 so now with me being the peggy again, it felt it was a waste of money as I would hardly be using them.

Newcastle Quay

After leaving Hull, the ship wasn't at sea for very long before we found ourselves back in the River Tyne. We went right up the river this time tying up at Newcastle Quay almost under Newcastle Bridge. Once again I busied myself making extra sandwiches with the gash breakfasts as well as the beef leftovers from lunch time. I didn't exactly sell the sandwiches or coffee to the dockers, but just made them up and hoped for a nice tip. However I couldn't help noticing just how poor some of those dockers were, how one or two of them would light up cigarette ends an inch long and even less. Some of the Geordie hatch workers offered me money but I didn't like taking it, in fact I thought I was financially better off than they were. I wasn't to make any extra money in Newcastle.

I had some good conversations with the dockers though, many of these people had themselves served in the Merchant Navy. They told me of some of the hard times they'd endured ten to twenty years earlier, some of the companies to steer clear of, and how lucky I was to be on such a nice ship. The average wage of these dock workers I was told, was about £8 a week.

That night I visited the fairground at North Shields; whilst there and after bumping into a few acquaintances, we watched a demonstration which brought back memories of Coronation Day, it was a one-man band show. I didn't tell any of my friends about the performance I'd given on Coronation Day, or I'd never have heard the last of it.

The bosun was always in an extra good mood when we were in port, and on the Saturday morning, July 11, he told me I could have the afternoon off. He also told me because he didn't want me wandering around in the dark, I must be on board by 23h00, then turn to at the normal time of 07h00 on the

Sunday. I grabbed the opportunity and decided to visit a friend in Blyth who himself was a bosun and one well into ship model making. Knowing the bus fare was eight pence each way for the sixteen mile journey, I took along one shilling and nine pence, the last of my financial resources. Amongst the money I had, was a shilling piece, eight pennies and two halfpennies. These halfpennies when highly polished, gave a silver appearance which to the unwary resemble shilling pieces; On the previous night, I'd tried unsuccessfully to pass them off to the stall holders in the fair ground.

I arrived at Blyth in the afternoon only to find my friend had gone to sea, so instead of the surprise meeting, I had a little wander around the town I knew so well. Outside the cinema, there was a man collecting donations for the restoration of the sailing ship *Cutty Sark*. He never recognised me, but I certainly recognised him. He was the same person who in previous times and as a civilian, had given religious instruction at the sea school. Shortly before he'd arrived at the sea school, the news from the galley wireless was a young person named Vivien had been engaged to give religious instruction. We all assumed this person named Vivien was a woman, a young woman, and the application list for those who wanted to attend the religious instruction was oversubscribed. It later transpired the religious teacher's name was indeed Vivien but not of the same gender which had been anticipated. Of course nobody wanted to continue with their 'being saved' on top of which was the fact Vivien turned out to be a most obnoxious person. After having proved to be most unpopular with the boys, his reign as a 'saviour' lasted about three or four weeks. "Would you like a shilling for your fund?" I asked the collector. "Oh that would be most kind of you," he replied in a warm and friendly voice I'd never heard before. He also had an unused smile which seemed to make his ugly face look even worse, I thought to myself how different people can be when they've got their hand out for something. With an air of aplomb and prosperity I dropped the polished half penny into his collection tin. His eyes lit up and he said my donation had been the most generous of the day. I walked away laughing, thinking how nice it would be to see his fat face when he opened the tin, then amongst his collection discovered, what would by then, have been a tarnished halfpenny.

After a while I decided that as the Newcastle bus was due I might as well return to the ship. I'd already ascertained from the ship's cook there was to be corned beef hash for tea, and I didn't want to miss out. Strolling away towards the bus stop, I ran my forefinger over the only two coins I had in my pocket, but then I stopped with a jolt, none of these coins had the milled edge of a shilling. On closer examination I discovered with horror, I had the two polished halfpennies: I'd dropped the real shilling in Vivien's collection tin.

It took me nearly three hours to do the sixteen miles back to Newcastle, I didn't mind the walk at all, and in fact I ran much of the way. What I did mind though was my being late for tea, but worse was to follow. When I arrived back on board at about 20h00 there was absolutely nothing left to eat in the hot press. I had to satisfy myself with cornflakes and water with some marmalade thrown in, but anything is better than nothing. It appeared everybody had gone ashore and although I knew there was a watchman somewhere I couldn't find him, just like the first day I'd joined, it seemed as though the ship was deserted.

Absolutely starving at about 22h30 I showered and turned in, it was just beginning to go dark. My cabin mate Fred and the bosun had gone ashore for the weekend as had some of the Geordies. The apparently deserted ship was quiet except for the occasional slapping of water against the ship's side and the berthing ropes creaking as they tightened then slacked off. I was just dozing off after the sixteen mile leg exercise, when through the open porthole I heard footsteps and voices coming from the main deck above; I realised right away these were women's voices, because they were accompanied by the stepping of high-heeled shoes. The footsteps continued into the accommodation then down the companionway and into the seamen's living quarters. At first I thought the women were with some of the sailors, then I heard them making inquiries as to whether there was anybody on board. My cabin door was on the hook and the next thing I knew was it being slipped off, the door flung open and the light turned on. With it being quite a warm night I was lying naked and all I had to cover me was a bed sheet, I sat up in my bunk rubbing my eyes to be confronted by two women. One of them stood in the doorway and to me looked quite haggard, the other one was behind her in the alleyway. "Hello Hinney, what are you doing on board all by yourself?" the haggard one asked as she took a step inside the cabin. Then with a giggle she asked, "Have you any space in your bed for me?" My impression was the lady was quite drunk, a fact soon borne out by the strong smell of wine or beer.

When I'd first joined the ship, my cabin mate Fred had warned me about having all our gear stolen from the cabin. He'd told me only personal friends should ever be allowed into the quarters and under no circumstances was I ever to allow anybody else in; these two reprobates were no doubt the unfavourable people he'd been referring to.

Well it was a bit of a shock to start with, however on having a closer look at the two ladies of the night, I found the nearest of them was quite old and probably over forty. She had dyed platinum hair, a face which was covered with rouge and lipstick, and an abundance of face powder to hide the bags under her eyes, she was doing all the talking. The other one was much younger and may well have been her daughter, anyway, I told them both to push off before the watchman came around. The older of the two noticing Fred's empty bunk, continued by saying there was plenty of room in the cabin for the three of us, and they had nowhere to sleep for the night. If I could, I'd have jumped out of my bunk and threw them both out of the accommodation but I was lying naked so I didn't bother.

By then the pubs must have closed, and I heard more footsteps coming along the main deck towards the after accommodation. They were the footsteps of two of the sailors.

When the two sailors descended the companionway and were faced by the two women, their joy knew no bounds. Within a short space of time, the sailors and the women had fallen in love with each other. They then made off to the cabin in which those two sailors were accommodated. A few minutes later and while I was still trying to come to terms with the unusual proceedings, one of those sailors came into my cabin. He was a bit drunk and ribbed me for squandering such a perfect opportunity of grabbing one, or even both of the women.

With the next morning being Sunday, the ship was still quite deserted of personnel; quite a few of the crew who lived locally had gone home for the weekend. On the lovely warm Newcastle morning and still famished with hunger, I was getting the breakfasts ready for those who'd slept on board. I suspected the two women were still on the ship, and I'd been careful enough to lock my cabin door otherwise I'd have incurred the wrath of Fred. During breakfast time where I took advantage of three of my missing shipmates by eating their meal, one of the sailors who'd entertained the promiscuous ladies came into the mess looking as though he hadn't slept. He asked me if I could please supply two extra breakfasts for his guests before they left the ship. I told him there were plenty of extra breakfasts in the hot press, but he must take them aft himself, as I didn't want to get into trouble from the bosun or Fred for serving them in the mess. Shortly after, I went down aft to make sure everyone knew breakfast was ready.

When I heard the showers running I went into the bathroom thinking some crew member or other was having an early morning rinse. On entering the bathroom I was quite surprised to see it was the two women who were in the showers. On seeing me at the doorway, the elder of the two and the one with the most to say, was standing naked and began laughing at me. She invited me to join her in the shower and give her back a rub. Being most unattractive with her wrinkled nipples almost touching her belly button, I told her she'd need an awful lot of money to get me in the shower with her, and ten times as much for me to bunk up with her. As a parting shot I asked would her wheelchair be still on the quayside where she'd left it. She didn't approve of my remarks and started screaming abuse at me by casting unsavory comments on the city of my birth, as well as the fact that I'd been born out of wedlock. In the adjoining shower the younger one stepped out to dry herself, she was quite nice looking and had a most attractive figure. She must have seen me wide eyed looking at her, so whilst drying herself then began flaunting her body in front of me, telling me what a good time I'd missed the night before; she then advised me not to be so shy if she came aboard that night.

Later on as I was clearing away in the mess room, I heard the two women walking up the starboard deck alleyway. This was the moment I'd been waiting for and went out on the deck to wish them goodbye. In my pocket I had a whistle from a lifeboat jacket which had been lying in the recreation room drawer; its sound resembled a policeman's whistle. As the two 'ladies' drew abreast of me at number four hatch, the elder of the two hurled a bit more abuse in my direction. I told her politely and advisedly she must be careful and hurry, because there were two policemen on the next ship and they were liable to come on board the *Willesden* at any moment. With that she gave me one last glare before hurrying down the gangway with her trainee accomplice. I leaned over the ship's side to see them go up the quay, then after they'd gone about 50 yards, I took the whistle from my pocket and blew it. The response from the two women was instantaneous, they both took off their high-heeled shoes, and surprised me with the speed at which they could run. I was in stitches laughing when the third mate Mr. Collister came out on the deck, he asked me who'd been blowing the whistle. I was still laughing when I handed the whistle over to him, explaining there'd been some young boys hanging around but I'd frightened them away. I didn't tell him of the two women who'd been aboard all night.

In comparison with the quiet weekend, Monday morning at Newcastle Quay was quite different, with all the hatches stripped cargo was already going down into the holds. I noticed the markings on some of the crates as to their various destinations, some of them marked for Genoa were stowed in the 'tween decks, while those for such places as Calcutta or Chittagong would be put at the bottom of the hold. Mr. Collister the third mate was on deck supervising, he later told me all the cargo stowage had to be planned in detail, so when we got to a certain port, the cargo for that particular port would be on top and easy to get at.

The deck crowd had all turned to, it was a lovely warm day with many of the sailors working stripped to the waist. Just before smoko I had a little wander around the decks. On venturing up to the focs'le head I saw John Coyne and Bill Houston splicing wire ropes; these I was told by Bill, were runner wires for the winches. He explained they were making Liverpool eye splices and asked me if I could do one. I told him I couldn't, saying in the sea school we'd been taught Admiralty splices but never the Liverpool splice. Bill explained the Admiralty splice should really be used on the runner wires, but it took too long to make one and while the ship was working cargo, runner wires were often in demand. The dockers who drove the winches treated the wires with great disregard and were forever breaking them, therefore, a quickly made Liverpool splice was necessary. It was quite fascinating watching the two sailors working in harmony, with the wire suspended from the deck-head, its formed eye was weighted down with a heavy shackle, then as the wire was spun, the lay was opened with the marlin spike and the tucks inserted. They done a really neat splice in just a few minutes. I remembered the splices I'd made in the sea school that took over two hours and weren't half as neat.

By that time it was smoko and as we walked down the deck Bill pointed to the four-inch foremast shrouds. He explained under their servings would be found a Liverpool splice, and in reality, only for standing rigging should a Liverpool splice be used.

At smoko, I had to contend with the remarks of the two sailors who'd entertained the two night-walkers on Saturday night. When I counteracted by saying the older woman should have been in a hospital for geriatrics, I was told amidst a chorus of laughs, "the older the fiddle the sweeter the tune." This no doubt meant old women were OK, but I'm afraid I wasn't impressed and couldn't understand how anybody could knock somebody off who was so old, especially when I later found out she was forty two. At lunch time I told Fred the whole story about the two women. He said I'd done the right thing by not allowing them in the cabin, such people were liable to steal everything in sight and disappear by the time I'd woke up.

I was most disappointed when we left Newcastle on Saturday July 18, not only because I had enjoyed myself in the city, it was because Bill Houston had missed the ship; Fred Hodges took his place in the eight to twelve watch. The weather was beautifully warm as we went down the River Tyne bound for London. The ship made twelve knots going down the North Sea where it was equally perfect weather and the sea like glass; it took two days to make it to the capital city.

In the River Thames, the bosun told me to go down in the engine room and ask the greaser or engineer for steam on deck to top the derricks. I always enjoyed going down below, where with regards to the greasers it was more like an old age home. First there's Old Bill who tried to convince everyone he was only fifty-five, however he also told everyone of the ships he'd been on at the turn of the century which was fifty-three years ago. If he told the truth in that respect, it either meant he was at sea when he was two years old or else he was telling little fibs. Then there was Old Albert who might have been telling the truth when he said he was sixty-one. Albert spent most of his spare time reading his bible, and would angry if anyone swore in his company. Everyone swore in the mess room. There was Old Fred who was once an AB on sailing ships, he was often to be heard talking about the hardships of being before the mast. Then there was Old George McIntosh who always liked a good moan and like Old Albert and John Coyne would happily join in with anybody who's having one. It has been said by the sailors, none of those four greasers would ever see sixty again, they all lied about their ages otherwise they would never have signed on a ship. Nevertheless, they were all apparently good at their jobs. Then there was young George, who is so called because he was only thirty-six, then Alan who was about the same age.

London

Early on July 20 the ship came alongside at the Victoria Docks in London; I was delighted to see Bill Houston waiting on the quayside. Later on in the day, he was logged two days pay for the time he'd been adrift; he said he was quite lucky, because if he'd still been on his previous ship the *Norton* of Chapmans, he'd have got an extra two days logging. I'd never been to London before, but to me it looked just like Liverpool or Newcastle with clouds of black smoke rising from funnels and chimneys. All this contributed to the grimy appearance of the area, and just as Dick Whittington had found out, the streets of London were not paved with gold. The dock we were in was full of ships from various companies, and I was having the various funnel markings pointed out to me. There were Shaw Saville's, Blue Star, Royal Mail, and a Furness Withy ship opposite us; there was also a P & O Liner *Strathnaver*, while astern of us was the Brocklebank ship *Malakand.*

At lunch time on Wednesday July 22, Captain Grist arrived on the quayside in his Morris 8 motor car; the chief steward and I were at the ship's side and watched him reverse his car into position. I liked the chief steward because although he was a senior figure on the ship, he was always open to conversation and someone I could talk to. He'd been gifted with a good sense of humour, and his sharp crafty eyes never missed a trick. At all times and wherever he was, his eyes would be darting furtively around in case he was missing out on something or other; someone in the mess had said he had more points than a porcupine.

As we stood there watching the captain maneuvering his motor car, I remarked to the chief if I ever got rich I'd have a motor car like the

captain. He told me he himself owned a motor car and it was at his home in Cardiff. I asked him what kind of a car did he have, he replied saying he'd just taken delivery of an SS Jaguar, one which was equipped with a radio in the walnut dashboard and a bar at the rear; I didn't know whether to believe him or not. The chief was one of those people who was never stuck for words and had the amazing ability to give an answer immediately to any question; it was as though he knew in advance what I was going to say and always had a witty reply ready.

It was quite a pleasure to have the London dockers use the mess room; Big Ron the cook gave me lots of extras, and I made them up into sandwiches. The dockers' foreman made sure I was well rewarded and ensured the mess room was always nice and clean. This gave me more time to drift around exploring, and made me think the bosun was right when he said there was extra money to be made. The sailors were all engaged in various tasks around the deck in the continuing warm weather. Tug Wilson and Gilly Smith, who joined the ship in Hull were over the bow on a stage, they were painting the ship's name both sides. John and Bill were doing rope work under the focs'le head, Fred was in the paint store, while the rest of the crowd were soojying. Under the focs'le head, I asked John Coyne would he believe the chief steward owned an SS Jaguar. "Why aye man, Hinney," he answered in his Geordie accent. "There's no such thing as a poor chief steward." He looked down at the hardened skin on his hands, and said he could once have been a steward, but regrettably turned the chance down.

I enjoyed walking around the ship watching the cargo going down the holds and the way the dockers stowed it. Although not much was seen of the bosun, I knew from past experience as soon as we were out at sea, he'd be around every corner waiting for me. At smoko on the second day in London, Mick Bayes an AB who had also joined the ship in Hull, approached me saying the ship astern of us was the *Malakand* out of Liverpool, and it had a full crowd of scousers on deck. He told me he'd only just been conversing with one of the Liverpool sailors who said they had a load of books on board, and someone should go around and collect them. I thought this was a good idea, and volunteered to go with the object of also having a good look around at the ship, then at the same time, to see if I knew anyone. I later walked along the quay, past the *Malakand*'s gangway and went right aft, sure enough there on the stern was the ship's name and port of registry, *Malakand* - Liverpool.

I walked up the gangway and onto the deck where amidst all the cargo handling and the hissing of steam winches I made my way aft. A strong smell of curry greeted me as I stepped over the coaming and into the accommodation. At the top of the companionway, an Indian approached me asking politely in his broken English could he be of help. I thanked him and said I was looking for the Liverpool sailors who had a stack of books for me to collect, and could he direct me to the deck department's accommodation. The Indian gave me a puzzled look, explaining there were no books to be had, and the ship's deck department were all from Calcutta. I felt a bit daft and immediately came to the conclusion Mick Bayes had set me up. When I got back to the *Willesden*, smoko was still in progress and Mick was delighted to have tricked me. The new crew which had signed on at Hull appeared to be a real happy-go-lucky crowd and it was a laugh a minute, although at that minute the laugh was on me.

When I'd finished cleaning up after teatime, Mick told me most of the deck crowd were going to the pub, and asked me if I'd like to go along too. I told him I was too young and I'd never been in a pub before, however the rest of the sailors were adamant I should accompany them.

Tug Wilson and Gilly Smith who also came from 'Ull on the River 'Umber then joined in and Gilly said, "If you don't come with us to the pub, we'll tell the bosun what you said behind his back." Well the truth was I hadn't said anything about the bosun, but Tug told lies and said he had witnesses. Having no alternative I agreed to go with them to the pub.

Soon after I started getting ready, Fred my cabin mate who was also going ashore with the bosun, asked me where was I off to. On telling him I was going to a pub with the rest of the sailors, he remarked saying he'd once heard me say I was never going to drink beer again. I told him I'd been forced to go by the sailors but if I didn't like the beer then I'd go to the cinema instead. I then discovered my pin stripe suit was getting too tight, Fred said it was with all the eating I was doing and the suit would never fit me when the trip was over.

As I was going up on deck, the bosun who was also in his go-ashore finery and waiting for Fred, was casting insulting aspersions on the chippy. "Why don't you go ashore you miserable old stay-aboard?" the bosun shouted. "What are you going to do with all that money when you die?" But the chippy who never got annoyed just grinned at him. (During the whole of the coming voyage, the chippy never once went ashore.)

At about 19h30 on a lovely warm evening, the deck crowd, with the exception of the bosun, Fred, Bill, and John, proceeded to the nearest pub in East Ham, it turned out to be 'The Roundhouse'. There weren't many people within and we took up the two tables on the far side, I was ushered into the corner and out of sight where I wouldn't be noticed. However, I'd only just got into position when the barman came over asking me who my teacher was at school; then he told me I was too young to drink and should leave the premises. Tug Wilson stood up saying he'd make sure I wouldn't be seen, and would take full responsibility should the police walk in; the barman thought about it, then agreed to let me stay. I had plenty of money thanks to my egg and bacon industry, but the crowd wouldn't let me pay for a round. I was still on my first pint when they were on their third or fourth

and the pub was starting to fill up; I felt a bit better now as I would not so easily be noticed in the crowd.

The music started and I was encouraged to drink a bit faster. People began dancing in the middle of the floor, then a group of four ladies sat on the next table to us. Everyone was in high spirits, the ladies on the next table to us got up and began dancing on the floor, much to the amusement of our company. After I'd finished my second pint I was feeling quite relaxed and happy. We'd been in the pub for about two hours by now, and the rest of the crowd must have had six beers each, but they all looked quite sober. More beer was placed in front of me, and although I was feeling a bit dizzy I was really enjoying the night. By now the floor was packed with dancers. Gilly Smith suggested I get up and dance with one of the ladies on the next table, I refused saying the barman would see me and throw me out. But then Mick whispered in my ear, one of the ladies kept looking at me, and he thought she had her eye on me. I couldn't help looking over at the next table, and there sure enough was one of its seated guests, a blue-eyed blonde smiling sweetly at me.

Once again I was goaded into getting up for a dance and was reminded about the chance I'd let slip by with the two women on Newcastle Quay. "I'm too young, they're all older than me," I said. Then I confessed I couldn't dance. "Can't dance?" said Mick. "You don't dance on a floor so packed as that, just stand up, grab a handful and move around."

By now the beer was taking its toll on me, I think it was Gilly who spoke across to the next table; he told the blue-eyed blonde I wanted to dance with her, but was too shy to ask. The blue-eyed blonde stood up smiling, beckoning me onto the dance floor where I staggered to the cheers of my shipmates from Hull. Coupled to the fact I was quite a bit drunk, I'd never had a dance before, and didn't know any steps; my dancing partner wore high heels which made her much taller than me. Blue-eyes put her arms around me and whispered she liked me because I was young, she liked young men and couldn't take her eyes off me all night; I felt quite flattered and even more so when she asked me to accompany her to her home for the night. By now my head was doing circles, the dance floor had emptied except for us two, and there was cheering and clapping from all around, even the barman who'd threatened to throw me out was joining in on the applause. Blue-eyes smelled as though she'd fell into a bath full of perfume as well as being heavily made up with facial cosmetics, but then beneath the make up I noticed the blued stubble of someone who shaved and the truth dawned on me. I went back to the table quite embarrassed to the unwanted ovation of my shipmates and those who were in the pub. The 'ladies' on the next table I later discovered, were stewards from a P & O Line ship and they were having a hen party because one of them was getting 'married' to one of the ship's firemen the next day.

I don't remember much about getting back to the ship, but the next morning I do remember having a huge hangover; it was much worse than the one I'd endured after Coronation Day. I was the centre of unwanted attention, even the dockers who had heard of my night in the pub were asking me for a dance. The bosun was in fine form and having observed the glazed look on my face kept at me all day; not much in the way of work was done, and he once again warned me as to my future conduct. I felt ill all day, but began to recover when working hours were over. As I was holding my head between my hands in the lunch hour, Gilly Smith said all I needed was another beer called a livener, but even the thought of beer in a smoke-filled pub made me feel sick again.

On sailing day from London, Captain Grist's motor car was loaded and stowed in the port side 'tween deck of number four hold, it was Fred Hodges who secured it. The rest of the crowd were busy in lowering derricks, battening down the hatches, and clearing up the decks in general. The sailors remarked on what a handy ship she was with just twelve five-ton derricks, and with no deck cargo it should be a pleasant outward voyage. The Blue Peter had been flying since morning time, I then saw the *Malakand* running her Blue Peter up. Inquiries revealed she was also bound for the Indian coast and being a faster ship would probably pass us in the English Channel. During the ship's stay in the UK I'd still spent a lot of time drawing, my hope was by the time we returned home, I'd be able to at least draw something.

Outward Bound

We let go from London on Friday July 24, the passage to Genoa was estimated to take eight days at eleven knots, assuming the weather was good. As usual the first thing which happens when past the three mile limit, is the chief steward opens the bond locker, then there's lifeboat and fire drill.

There is also a big wash down to rid the ship of the accumulated dirt which has littered the decks and to give the ship a fresh appearance. This washing down takes place each time the ship leaves port as well as every Saturday morning at sea. Also on Saturday mornings the decks are scrubbed and holystoned. When washing down takes place with the fire hoses, someone in the washing down party has to go around the whole ship to ensure all the port holes are battened down. This is to make sure no compartment or cabin is flooded out. I'm glad it wasn't me who was sent on the errand because one of the engineers cabins in the port alleyway got drenched.

I'd been listening to the sailors talking about the dreadful weather which could be expected in the Bay of Biscay, and hoped we'd have a repeat of the heavy weather we'd previously experienced in the North Atlantic; this would then excuse me from scrubbing out. During the time when the ship was being thrown all over the place, it seemed I was the only one on the ship who'd enjoyed the bad weather. This was partly because the mundane jobs of the peggy had been temporarily halted; also because I enjoyed the spectacle. I recalled the past couple of months which had mostly been quite a happy experience for me, however, with the assistance of the bosun things were soon to change. He told me he'd been noticing how I'd improved in my working times and he had a nice little surprise for me. I stuck my chest out a little and thought, 'Praise from the bosun is praise indeed.' At first I wondered what the little surprise was, but was very soon to unpleasantly find out.

During the next day when we were in the English Channel, John Cunningham was promoted from deck boy to JOS; once again I was the lowest form of life in the deck department. John was obviously happy about his promised promotion but even happier about the pay rise he would get with it. His pay was increased from £10 a month to £15-10-0, a rise of 55%. Amongst all the shipping going both ways in the English Channel, the *Malakand* passed us on the port side at breakfast time. She must have been making a good fourteen knots because she'd left us out of sight after about three hours. After I'd cleaned up from lunch and showered at 13h00, I was just getting ready to do some drawing in the recreation room when the bosun arrived on the scene. He had hold of a bucket and scraper which he presented to me saying, I was the one who said I wanted to work on deck so now I was to get my chance. He led me to the winch at number six hatch informing me I was to scrape the underneath clean as well as under all the steam pipe casings. With a glint in his eyes he said for me the holiday was over, and for the rest of the trip on each working day, I was to turn to on deck from 13h00 to 15h00. He further told me all the winch beds on the ship were to be done, "Shipshape and Bristol fashion," one a day he said, and they must be so clean when I'd finished he could eat his dinner off them. The mystery of the nice little surprise had now been unfolded.

I didn't particularly like cleaning winch beds, trapped underneath was grease and broken bottles, newspapers, beer cans, and all kinds of rubbish. I thought as I was scraping and cleaning, this accumulation of rubbish must have been there for years not just months, and never before had they been cleaned. It was most amazing to think after all the weather we'd had in the North Atlantic the rubbish hadn't been washed away. There was so little space for me to work cleaning the winch beds, it made me think I was probably the only one on deck who was small enough to do the job. At the same time, I thought if I had a job getting down to clean underneath, who besides me would be able to inspect my work? By 15h00 I'd cleaned the winch bed and all the steam pipe casings around it, I then disposed of all the debris right aft. The bosun who never seemed to be far away inspected the work, and with a big smirk on his face gave his approval.

At tea time and being hungry I got another shock when I went into the galley, there in a big kit was some foul smelling concoction which to me resembled cow flop. I looked at and asked, "What's that Doc?" Big Ron gave a laugh saying it was beef curry, I couldn't bear to smell the stuff let alone eat it. I told the ship's cook nobody in the mess would ever eat it; but how wrong I was, not only did the crowd eat it all, but asked me to go and see if there was any more. I had to be content with eating bread and jam, then found out to my horror curry would be served once a week. The only consolation for me, was each time there was to be curry, the cook told me he'd also make steam duff which he knew was my favourite. However July 29 1953 was not a happy day for me.

Later on I told Bill of the new ordeal I had to face in cleaning the winch beds between 13h00 and 15h00. When I told him I now had to work eleven hours a day, non-stop from 07h00 until 18h00, and then a bit more as well, he told me it was the normal routine on all ships for the peggy to work between 13h00 and 15h00. He said I shouldn't complain, I wouldn't be a peggy forever. He went on to say if I worked my times right I could have a breakfast hour plus a lunch hour, by eating with the seven-bell men.

We passed Ushant, the northern most side of 'The Bay', the skies were blue and except for the disturbance the ship made there was hardly a ripple on the water. There was to be no hoped for heavy weather, therefore, I had to continue the peggying and the cleaning of the winch beds. On the second day of my 'working on deck', Mick Bayes and John Dick who were the watch on deck were having it nice and easy soojying. Paddy Dolan was on the wheel, Fred was working under the focs'le head and I had the worst job of all scraping the opposite winch bed by number six hatch.

At 15h00 when the bosun came around to inspect my work, I don't know how he done it, but he must have got right down on his hands and knees and found a bit I'd missed. The bosun was strutting around like the lord of the manor and I thought how nice it would be, if after about ten years and I was a bosun, he came on board as one of the deck crowd, and the winch beds required cleaning.

Next day I began on number five winches. This was to be really difficult because of all the deck obstructions around the winch which included steam pipe casings, sounding pipes and the after end of number five hatch. The starboard side winch bed was packed with all kinds of rubbish much more than the port one, but once again I cleared it away, or should I say 'some' of it. I knew the bosun would never be able to get down and inspect my work owing to his rather large posterior, so after having reported to him I'd finished, I emptied what trash I'd collected before going down aft to shower.

At about 15h30 I was in the recreation room all nice and clean and just about to start drawing pictures when the bosun came in. His eyes were blazing, and he bellowed, "I thought you said you'd cleaned the winch bed at number five. It's filthy!" He screamed, "Now get out of here and do the job properly." He angrily left the room and I had to get back into my dirty clothes and get stuck in again. I just couldn't help wondering how on earth a man so broad as him, could get down so far underneath the winch bed to discover my sins.

We passed Finisterre and I continued doing half an hour on the wheel each evening before going up on the focs'le to learn the lookout after dark; this was the first time I saw dolphins, and what a beautiful sight they made. As the ship surged forward at its ten or eleven knots, they would swim ahead; then sometimes with a burst of speed, race away at what must have been well over thirty knots before returning to lead the ship. I found it was much easier to do the lookout than steer the ship, it was also nice to talk to the lookout man learning all the time about the life on board this and other ships. I was aware when I was in the mess room with all the sailors, I couldn't join in their conversation because I didn't know anything about ships and didn't have anything in common with them. On the lookout things were different where the man there was glad for anybody to talk to, and it was really the only time anybody listened to me.

I seemed to get on OK with the people on the ship, but always got an unfriendly reception from the second steward; he gave the cabin boys the same treatment. Each day before breakfast I had to collect the dry stores from the second steward who often went out of his way to keep me waiting. I was always on a tight schedule, and when I went down into the store room I'd often be kept waiting for ten minutes for the stores. I then received the daily tea, sugar and coffee ration for nineteen men which really was rationed out. The second steward was a real tight-fisted company's man, he always weighed the stores right down to the last ounce with never any extra; in fact I had to correct him on a number of occasions for not giving me the full whack. He'd mastered the art of 'hurling' the tea or sugar onto the weigh scale, then as soon as the weigh scale dipped slightly, he'd quickly lift it off, but I'd seen this little grocer's trick before and wasn't to be fooled. He didn't like to be corrected or told he was wrong and because he knew I was on a tight schedule, he'd punish me by making me wait each day for the stores.

At one time, I had on his advice left the ration tins outside the storeroom, carried on with my work and had the cabin boy deliver the dry stores to me. This was an excellent arrangement, or would have been until I soon found out he'd shortchanged me by about an ounce of tea each time this procedure took place. The arrangement was abandoned. To save time, I asked him if it would be possible to draw a full week's ration of tea and sugar, by which token I'd save a lot of time each morning and at the same time would spare him the necessity of issuing the stores. This request was refused point blank. It later dawned on me, in the hot weather not so much tea or coffee is drunk as in normal times, there would then be a surplus of stores in the mess. By issuing the stores daily the second steward would profit on the days I never bothered going for them; but on the advice of the sailors I made sure I collected the stores every single day. Although the board of trade scale was one tin of condensed milk every ten days, we received a tin once a week, but this was no thanks to him. The rest of the stores went to the galley. In the saloon pantry they had evaporated milk, a luxury known as 'shakey' milk but this little item like so many others was denied to the crew's mess.

On the next day between 13h00 and 15h00 I began on the fourth winch bed on the port side, this one wasn't so bad, but nevertheless I made a good job of it to avoid later retribution. As I was cleaning the underneath, I wondered again just how the bosun, in searching for poor workmanship, had discovered my previous day's folly. Old Albert came along the deck on his way to the engine room, and when he saw me scraping under the winch beds fuming and cursing, he told me if I thought cleaning winch beds was a dirty job, it was absolutely nothing, compared to when the greasers had to clean the scavengers in the engine. He had a good moan about us younger generation saying how easy life was for us; before telling me of the terrible times he'd had at my age. I was almost in tears when he told me he had to work a twelve hour day, as well as the blood hours, in the days before overtime payment had been invented.

At 15h00 I duly reported to the bosun saying the winch bed was clean and departed aft, however I didn't go for a shower. Instead I went and hid behind the water tank on top of the poop housing, from there I would be able to observe the bosun doing his inspection of my afternoon's work. Imagine my surprise when he came around ten minutes later to look under the winch bed. I thought he was going to get down on all fours to peer underneath, more than anything I just wanted to see how a person so plump as him could do so when someone even my size found it a bit of a squeeze. The bosun did no such thing! Instead, the crafty swine who was fast becoming my enemy number one, had a mirror attached to a broom handle and searched with ease the whole underneath of the winch frames and the steam pipe casings.

In the evening watch I was given some canvas from Gilly Smith, he said he'd show me how to make a kitbag and a peaked cap like the bosun had; so after I'd finished in the mess we started cutting out all the pieces in the recreation room. Gilly said he was going to supervise all my work, and he wanted seven locking stitches to the inch, and if I took my time I should have the cap made in a few days and the kitbag finished long before we arrived back to the UK. Next day I was given some bits of engine gasket from Old Albert and after three nights I had a peaked cap like the bosun, it wasn't as good as his though, which made me think he'd bought his from a shop.

Through the Med.

Five days after leaving London we passed Gibraltar, the weather by now having become markedly hot. Having cut the legs off my dungarees to make a pair of shorts, I'd been advised to keep the legs so when we were homeward bound and the weather cold, I could sew them back on again. Next day, an altercation between Ron Stafford the cabin boy and myself took place. There had been a previous encounter when I'd seen him mopping out the alleyway and remarked to him as the bosun had once said to me, "Only stewards and old women use mops," and this started it off. It so happened the stewards were allowed off from 13h00 until 15h00 because they started work at 06h00 as well as working their lunch hour. At about 14h00 and after having been to the pantry for a drink of water, I went through the mess then down the alleyway in which the stewards were accommodated. There I almost tripped over an empty bucket which had been left outside the door. Ron Stafford came out of his cabin with a towel around him threatening to brain me for spoiling his siesta. A bit of shoving and pushing from each of us resulted in Peter Kingham the second cook coming out of his cabin and breaking up what was nearly a fight, but the seeds were set for further conflict. What I noticed about the use of mops, was they never cleaned in the corners. A scrubbing brush did, and on this point the bosun was right, but personally I myself would rather use a mop.

By the time we reached Genoa on Saturday August 1, I was still on the winch beds having only the four on the foredeck left to do; I wondered what other little treat the bosun had in store for me when they were all finished.

Whilst we were in Genoa I made an amazing discovery. Whilst emptying the teapot, I found the gash bucket in the pantry was full. Therefore, and because I was under pressure to make some fresh tea quickly, I put the old tea leaves on a tray and hid them under the hot press out of the way; then I forgot all about the tea leaves and the tray until the next morning. When I did retrieve them from under the hot press, I found they'd all shrivelled up with the overnight heat, giving once again the appearance of fresh tea leaves. Telling the crowd about my discovery in case they used them by mistake, I began saving them in a sack. The plan being when the sack was full, I would sell them in the Suez Canal to the gentry of the region of whom I had heard so much about.

We weren't to stay long in Genoa and no subs were given out. Fortunately I still had some money from my egg and bacon sales in London, and went ashore with John Levitt the other cabin boy. I liked Genoa, the people were so friendly and it was a pity our stay had to be so short. It so happened there were a few long faces in the mess because we'd been in port for the weekend; a Sunday at sea would have resulted in an extra day's leave. As the ship made her way down the Tyrrhenian Sea, I was on the first of the fore-deck winch beds. At about 14h55 and after having reported to the bosun I'd finished the afternoon's work, I went to the pantry for a drink of water. I was walking nice and quietly down the so-called stewards alleyway when Ron Stafford came charging out of his cabin, his fists raised, and without warning a fight started. After a scuffle he threw a punch at me and I returned the compliment. In doing so I caught him with my left fist on his protruding molar tooth. The fight didn't last long because Big Ron came out of his cabin and grabbed the two of us. He had my neck in one of his hands and Ron Stafford's in the other and tried his best to shake the living daylights out of the two of us. He seemed quite amused by the fiasco, then after talking to us, suggested we both shake hands, which we did. From then on Ron and I became the best of friends. Somehow the bosun found out about the fight but he wasn't amused like Big Ron was. He said people on ships don't fight, then he told me although the stewards passage in question was a working alleyway, I mustn't use it in future between 13h00 and 15h00.

At 20h30 I went up on the focs'le head, Bill Houston was the lookout and I showed him my injured left hand which was lacerated. He told me I should have gone to see the chief steward for a dressing, he said in this hot weather cuts went septic very quickly. I replied saying I'd had a lot worse before, and didn't want to incur the wrath of Mr. Perkins by wasting his time with such a minor injury.

There was a ship on the starboard bow and I took great pleasure in giving the focs'le bell one ring, this would alert the officer on watch there was shipping in the area. The officer of the watch would then come out on the wing of the bridge and acknowledge the reported ship by calling, "Thank you," on other occasions he would flash the Aldis lamp. Two rings on the bell meant there was a ship on the port side, whilst three rings indicated a ship right ahead. This series of bell ringing from the lookout was standard practice on all Merchant Navy ships; land, lighthouses or any other objects are reported in the same manner.

By the time I awoke next morning my lacerated left hand had become badly swollen, I showed it to the bosun who said I must report to the chief steward who put a bandage on it. He told me to keep the wound dry, and come back the next morning for another dressing. Later in the day I was pumping up the galley water with my good right hand, when Captain Grist who was out on deck approached me. "What's the matter with your hand young man?" he asked. Being caught unawares, I replied, "I caught it on a rusty marlin spike sir." The captain gave me a look which told me he didn't believe me.

On the following day my left hand had swollen to the size of a cabbage, the chief steward redressed the wound saying I must see the doctor on our arrival at Port Said. During the morning smoko, I was walking from aft to amidships and went up the port side. Sitting outside on number five hatch also having their smoko, were the junior engineers. They were all in their early twenties and were having a good laugh about something or other. I'd always been on good talking terms with the juniors, and on my approach they called me over still laughing at whatever it was. I was soon to learn, one of them had been seduced by a fifty-four year old woman whilst the ship had been in South Shields, and my opinion was sought as to whether I would have let such a thing happen to me. I immediately thought of the two night walkers who'd boarded the vessel in Newcastle and asked, "Was she blonde?" The peals of laughter got louder as one of them said, "No she was a greyish-white." The engineer who had been involved in the South Shields incident, had a sheepish look about him and hid his face behind his hands. Then they questioned me about my injured hand. It was then I discovered they'd all heard about the fight with the cabin boy, I thought back to the look of disbelief on the captain's face when I'd answered his question.

In the evening we passed Stromboli a small volcanic island twenty-five miles north of Sicily. All hands came out on deck to witness the amazing phenonomen of the lightning, which is a feature of the area. It certainly was something to see, huge sheets of lightning lit the sky and quite often the flashes were so prolonged and bright, it was just like day light. A couple of hours later the ship passed through the narrow Straight of Messina, there we had mainland Italy on the port side and Sicily to starboard.

The Suez Canal

By the time we arrived at Port Said on August 7, not only had my left hand become useless, but my forearm was now badly swollen. The red veins were protruding from it and the chief steward seemed quite concerned. However, from the unsympathetic bosun I was still found work to do with my good right hand.

We anchored outside Port Said Harbour, where the area abounded with Arab fishing dhows and quite a few of them were under our stern wanting 'changey for changey'. There were also a few more ships awaiting the south-bound convoy. Abeam of us a few hundred yards away on the starboard side was the cruiser HMS *Gambia*. The warship looked quite stylish in a way, she had two vertical funnels and obviously having been built for the Second World War she wasn't built to be a beauty, but to me there was something about her that gave the impression of elegance. Our gangway was lowered on the starboard side and a launch from the cruiser came over to our ship, two of its ratings were then led to the captain's cabin where they probably signed or exchanged documentation.

The doctor then came out with the ship's agent who also brought the mail, I was summoned to the chief steward's cabin where the 'quack' was to administer treatment to my hand. On waiting outside I was joined by another of the deck crowd who was also to receive treatment. "What's the matter with you that you need the quack?" I asked, thinking he also had some minor injury. The sailor replied, "I've come for a jab." I looked at him puzzled and asked him why did he need one. He then told me, "To get rid of the dose." It took a while for the penny to drop before I asked him, "Where did you catch your packet, in London?" He shook his head. "Didn't you know?" he replied. "I caught it in Newcastle, the night those two women tried to get into your bunk." I was shocked and silent for a while as my mind went back to the night at Newcastle Quay. Still quite taken aback, there was another shock to come when I exclaimed, "I wouldn't have let that ugly old thing in my bunk for a year's pay." He laughed a bit and told me, it wasn't the old one he'd bunked up with, but the young one; his cabin mate who'd acquired the services of the older one was OK. Still quite flabbergasted, I told him I felt sorry for his misfortune, he in turn told me he was sorry he'd had a laugh at me, using me for the butt of his jokes for not having bedded down with one of them. He admitted it served him right and also told me his 'packet' had surfaced a week previously.

When the doctor treated me, I had to lay on the chief's settee, and got the needle which was about three inches long in my right buttock, and didn't it just hurt. Mr. Perkins then gave me another dressing on my injured hand telling me he'd spoken to the bosun telling I was to be put on light duties. I went to the bosun and told him I was to do light duties until my hand got better but all this did was to give him a good belly laugh. He looked at me and said, "OK I'll give you the easiest and lightest work on the ship – go and do the peggy's job."

The flies at sea were bad enough, now they were everywhere relishing the Egyptian heat and trying to get under my bandage. With the derricks topped, the ship later went into Port Said anchoring right opposite the port office where the Union Jack flew on top; there were also quite a number of British Army and RN personnel present on the parade ground. On the way in Bill Houston showed me the statue of De Lessops on the breakwater, he was the Frenchman who had engineered the building of the Suez Canal. Number three and four hatches were stripped and a cargo of potatoes and other Egyptian exports were being stowed in the 'tween decks.

Due to the ship working cargo, there were dozens of Arabs on the deck, most of them were unauthorised and came aboard to make their living one way or another. I was quite amused at their attire of shifts which looked like night shirts and their big baggy pants. On mentioning this to sarcastic Old Albert, he told me they were probably just as amused at my mode of dress.

The deck crowd then loaded four boats onto the deck, two on the foredeck port and starboard, then two on the afterdeck port and starboard. The purpose of these boats, was in case the ship had to tie up in the canal. There were also eight boatmen to accompany these boats, and each of them had their boats full of merchandise which they hoped to sell to the crew. I remembered the advice that old Bill Orbell had given me a few days previously when he said, I should be careful when buying off the bum boats which came alongside; or the boatmen who came on the ship. Whilst we were loading the potatoes a barge came alongside which was owned by George Roby, he was the leading bum boatman in Port Said, there were others called 'Steam on Deck' one called 'Rifle-Eye' and a few more the crowd knew of.

At the time there was a lot of activity going on up forrard with the chippy working on a big box on the focs'le head. I don't know whether he'd made the box or whether it had come from ashore on a barge; there was also a big searchlight which accompanied the box. A number of Arabs were also busy on the focs'le, they were assisting in putting the box over the stem of the ship using the single davit which was right up in the eyes of the ship. I'd always wondered what the davit on the focs'le was for. Later on they loaded the searchlight into the top of the box before connecting all the electric wires. This searchlight was to be used for navigating the ship while she was steaming through the canal in the hours of darkness.

I found all the unauthorised Arabs on deck had something to sell, and all had a disarming smile on their faces. At first every one of the Arabs I spoke to asked me where I came from; after I'd told them I came from Liverpool, they excitedly told me their father or some other of their ancestors had originated from there. I was offered 'solid gold' necklaces, crucifixes, bangles, rings, and lots of Egyptian souvenirs, but fortunately and for the past few weeks I'd been well warned by my shipmates of the devious and various approaches which would be made to encourage a sale. After examining one item of 'gold' which even had a hallmarks on it, I told its seller who was a boatman named Mustapha, his goods were a most remarkable bargain, unfortunately I was without money. He then suggested I go and steal something – some money or a watch from my shipmates – anything to the value, which could then be used in exchange for his goods. Everybody had Spanish Fly for sale.

Then there was another who ushered me out of sight to the engine room alleyway. First he had a good look around to make sure he wasn't to be apprehended, then from underneath his shift he brought out and showed me a 'solid silver' statuette which he said was worth £50. He told me he'd stolen it from a rich man's house and because he was in such a hurry to escape the vicinity and the police, it was going at the bargain price of £2. I told the vendor I only had £1, then after some haggling, he agreed to reduce the price to £1. Then I told him I'd made a mistake and I only had 10/- at which point the owner of the 'silver' statue broke off negotiations. It appeared one of the main selling points of the locals, was to sell their goods as 'stolen property'; this must have added some kind of spicy incentive to a sale. Numerous people in Port Said approached me during the day, and they all seemed to be selling some kind of stolen goods. The next one who asked me where I came from was given the answer I lived in South Shields, he then told me he had many relatives in South Shields.

While the crowd was working and because of my inability to do so, the bosun had told me to guard the after accommodation; this was to discourage any unauthorised people from wandering around it. The port side door was locked and every porthole battened down. My orders were quite simply to make sure nobody except crew members went through the starboard door. Therefore, I just locked the door I was guarding and sat on the bitts watching the numerous 'salesmen' trying to gain entry. I had a good laugh when Fred my cabin mate came along the deck. Upon asking one of the loiterers why he was hanging around the accommodation; Fred was told he wanted to use the toilet and wash his hands. Before chasing him away, Fred, with his rather dry sense of humour, asked if he knew how to use a toilet rather than a sand-dune, and would he like to take his mobile dandruff with him.

Later on, Old Bill came along the deck with an important looking smartly dressed Arab salesman who was a collar and tie job. He was in the process of selling Bill a bottle of whiskey, and I unlocked the door for them to go below and tie up the deal. A few minutes later the salesman emerged on deck having made his sale and left the ship. I was at the time standing directly over Old Bill's cabin looking over the side when I saw the same whiskey bottle I'd just seen, getting thrown out of the porthole, with a 'sploosh' it hit the water and sank. It didn't take much, even for me, to realise poor Old Bill had been sold a bottle of cold tea, and after him warning me not to fall for any trickery in the Suez Canal. When he later came up on deck his face was rather aghast, I didn't tell him I'd seen the bottle going over the wall, I didn't tell anybody else either.

Saturday August 8, on the way through the canal it was extremely hot and especially in the cabin. I remarked on this to Fred, who said I should just wait until we get in to the Red Sea and then I'll find out what heat really is. As well as drinking a lot of water in this hot climate, I'd also been drinking a lot of fruit juice which cost three shillings and four pence a bottle – half a day's pay. This was noticed by the chief steward who warned me I was spending too much on chocolate and fruit juice, and by the time the trip was over I'd have no pay off. We stopped at Ismalia to pick up some additional potato cargo before anchoring in the Bitter Lakes with the rest of the convoy. The fact we anchored, allowed the north-bound ships to pass. Some of the crowd went for a swim, but I was unable to because of my hand. Anchor was raised at midnight and the ship proceeded to Port Tuefiq where we arrived on Sunday morning. There we stopped for an hour or so and three of the boats and their valiant crews left the ship.

The Red Sea

On sailing from Port Teufiq at about noon, the remaining boat was to be given a tow for a few miles, this was to save the boatmen rowing to their final destination. The boat was now in the water under the stern and made fast to the ship's bitts. Mr Brown the second mate who was on the after deck, gave the boatmen permission to take a tow. He told me I was to stand by the bitts and let their line go when they gave the signal; Mr. Brown then went on the bridge to do his watch. The ship began moving with the line between ship and boat growing taut, the two boatmen were waving to me to show their appreciation of getting a free tow.

I waved back to Mustapha, the one who had suggested I steal my shipmates' belongings and the waving continued as the ship picked up speed. I had previously noticed their boat was made fast on their end, with the eye then a couple of turns around the stag horn. In such circumstances they couldn't slip and would have to either cut the rope or wait until I was ready to let them go. I admired the new four-inch grade one manila rope which was probably worth more than the boat and wondered from where they'd acquired it. The waving and exchanges of niceties continued, then after about fifteen minutes they gave the signal to let go. Maybe I thought they were still waving to me or possibly I misinterpreted their frantic appeals to let go – anyway I went for a little walk around the deck.

About ten minutes later I had another look over the stern, the two boatmen were frantically screaming about something. By now there was a bit of a swell and their boat was bouncing up and down in the wake of the ship. The land was beginning diminish and I was in stitches laughing, realising if they cut their rope they'd lose about fifty fathoms of it. Just then

Old Albert arrived on the scene with his bible in hand, when he saw the frantic appeals of the boatmen he slipped their line and gave me a telling-off. As he was doing so, the apprentice Alistair Kerr came aft telling me the second mate wanted me on the bridge. Realising the second mate knew of my failure to carry out his instructions, I was a bit nervous as I made my way to the bridge. On my arrival, he asked me why I hadn't let the boatmen go when they requested, I told him I thought they were just waving to me. He sent me away warning me not to let such a thing happen again, but I could see a twinkle in his eyes. (A few days later Alister Kerr the apprentice told me the second mate had watched the whole incident and was highly amused.)

In the Red Sea the weather was very hot, the temperature in the accommodation was so high and unbearable nearly everyone slept on deck. Some slept on number six hatch, some on the deck beside it, others around the poop, while the stewards were all on number five hatch.

By the next morning everyone in the mess had heard about the misunderstood signals from the boatmen: jokingly some of them said it was a shameful thing I had done to two poor boatmen who were just trying to make their living. Of course they all agreed on the ship's return to the Suez Canal, the same boatmen would be on the ship and I was in big trouble. I told those in the mess, one of the boatmen called Mustapha had suggested I go and steal money and watches from the cabins, but that just brought a howl of laughter as nobody had any money or owned a watch.

By the time of our arrival at Port Sudan on Tuesday night, my hand had made an excellent recovery. We went in at first light on Wednesday August 12. The weather was so hot, even before breakfast time the heat was upon us. The derricks had been topped, the hatches opened and cargo began being discharged. We were one of only two ships in the port, the other being an American Victory Ship.

After I'd scrubbed the mess out and to keep it clean, the bosun told me to lock it up saying it was too hot to have smoko indoors, and from now on it would be on number four hatch. At 13h00 the bosun brought me up to the focs'le head and directed me to take the appropriately numbered awnings down from the shelves and carry them aft. Under the focs'le head it was like being inside an oven it was so hot; in the lunch hour I must have drunk a gallon of water, but by now it had all come out in sweat. The canvas awnings were so big and heavy, then combined with the terrific heat I was left almost limp. I just wasn't strong enough to get them down off the shelves. Fortunately at the time, Fred was next door in the lamp room and he gave me a hand to get them down and out on the deck. Gilly and Tug were also around on the fore deck and they helped me take them aft. Bill Houston and John Coyne were there to put them up and I was to help. He often showed me things did Bill, this time he taught me how to set awnings, reminding me the lanyards which go around the ridge wire must be no more than a fathom long and secured with a slip clove hitch. The reason for this he went on, was if a storm suddenly blew up, they could more easily and quickly be taken down. Paddy Dolan and Curly Megginson did the awnings on the bridge, John Dick and John Cunningham the boat deck, and soon after, the awnings were up all over the ship. The Sudanese hatch men working the cargo were a strangely mild-mannered race of people, unfortunately they were also very poor. After each meal they would wait on deck outside the pantry in the hope there were some leftovers. I gave them what I could, and was pleased at the way they all waited in an orderly fashion; I was amazed at the way each would take a fair share of what was on offer, sometimes this was very little.

At breakfast time on the third day I was to witness what was to me a very strange incident. After having placed the leftovers tray on number four hatch, I was feeling quite pleased I could make someone happy for a change. None of the waiting Sudanese spoke English, but they all gathered around the tray muttering and looking suspiciously at the gift of food, suddenly one of them excitedly shouted something, then they all ran away screaming. They all kept their distance at the other side of number three hatch from where I was given the most unpleasant looks; none of them would come near the tray and I was absolutely flabbergasted. While all this was going on, Captain Grist who was on the after end of the captain's deck had his movie camera out, I watched him filming the whole incident. Through an interpreter, I later discovered, I'd offended the Sudanese hatch workers by offering them bacon with the left over breakfast and their religion forbade them from eating such food. Later on, and even after I'd thrown the bacon into the gash bucket, they still wouldn't take the eggs or bread which had been on the tray, because they'd been contaminated by having been on the same tray as the bacon. During smoko the chief steward chanced by and I remarked the captain had filmed me with his cine camera. I said I'd love to see myself on film just to see what I looked like. Mr. Perkins replied saying he also had a cine camera, unfortunately, he'd left it at home, however if I were to come back on the next trip he'd take some films and show them on his projector. I told Mr. Perkins that I didn't believe he had all those things like an SS Jaguar, a cine camera and a projector and his own house, but he just sniggered at me and showed me his gold wrist-watch.

Later on in the day I was working on the foredeck; I'd lost or mislaid my home-made cap and my head was covered by a makeshift hat which had been fashioned from a piece of cloth from the rag-bag. Due to the intense heat and to cool me down, I soaked my headgear under the fire hydrant then covered my head with it. Mr. Collister the third mate, who was supervising the discharging at number one and two hatches saw me do this, and came running over grabbing the cap from my head. He warned me what I'd just done was the best way to get sunstroke, it was the first time I'd ever seen him angry.

I didn't like Port Sudan because it was so hot, dry, and dusty; there was nowhere to go, except to the Missions to Seamen, or the 'Flying Duck' as it was referred to; this place was about thirty yards away from the gangway. During our stay there, the vicar, who the crowd called the 'sky pilot' came on board for prayers which Old Albert thoroughly enjoyed; we were then invited to see a film show in the mission. The crew of the American ship also attended the show, and the vicar's daughter operated the projector; the film was all about the missionaries in Africa, and I think Old Albert loved it. The next morning the vicar's daughter hung all her underwear out on the line for all of us to see, but judging by what we'd seen of her nobody was very excited.

The water in the dock was about fifty feet deep where the ship was berthed, this water was so clear the bottom could be seen, there were beautifully coloured fish swimming around and I put a fishing line over using a piece of bacon for bait. The fish couldn't have been the same religion as the hatch workers because it wasn't long before I pulled a fish out of the water; the strangest fish I could have ever imagined. It wasn't a very big fish, probably twelve inches long, but its teeth were just like those of a human being, even its face had a human appearance to it. Tug Wilson put the blade of his knife in it's mouth, and it bit with such ferocity it left an indent on the steel blade; the hook was somehow removed from its mouth before it was released back into the water

We left Port Sudan for Aden on the fifteenth, it was nice to get out into the open sea again where although the intense heat continued, the number of flies decreased. The ship was making its usual eleven or twelve knots, and standing on the open deck one would think there would be a twelve-knot wind, but it wasn't so. Instead, the ship seemed to be in a kind of vacuum as it moved forward dragging all the atmosphere with it. The only place anywhere on the ship where there was any kind of a breeze, was in the deck alleyways, although it was an extremely hot breeze. There was absolutely nowhere on the ship except maybe the freezer that wasn't stiflingly hot.

There were no cold water taps anywhere on the ship, even the captain didn't have one, the only places this luxurious commodity could be obtained was the little fridge in the saloon pantry or the meat freezer. One of my jobs as peggy on collecting the morning dry stores, was to take a bucket of fresh water down to the freezer room. Then at lunch time after the cook had opened the freezer for the next day's meat supply, I'd bring it up again for the crowd to have a drink of cold water. This was the only time in the day we ever got a cold drink, the rest of the time it was water from the pantry tap, which even at night was quite warm. If on the other hand the drinking water tap was left to run long enough, cool water would come up from the tanks; but I'd been caught doing this a number of times for which I was always given a stern rebuke.

Wasting water on a ship is a thing that nobody of experience will tolerate. Even whilst having a shower I'd been advised to first wet myself down, turn the shower tap off, then after soaping myself down, quickly rinse off. This method of showering used up less than half a bucket of water. Because of the huge difference in the usage of fresh water, there are always showers and never baths on ships, at least not for the crew. It was the older hands on the ship who were most concerned about the saving of water, and when I asked Old Bill Orbell why was there such a fuss, he just shrugged his shoulders. He said old habits die hard and it just wasn't the done thing, not even in port. He told me of an experience he'd once had after his ship had been sunk during the war, the crew had taken to the boats where they remained for two weeks, the most precious thing in that boat was water.

In the afternoon I was in the after accommodation where I said to Old George McIntosh I'd give anything for a nice drink of cold water. A few moments later he came out of his cabin and gave me a glass of water which I put to my mouth, it was deliciously cool and I drank the lot. I asked Old George from where did he get such lovely cold water in this blistering heat, whereon taking me to his cabin he showed me his 'chatti'. This was an ordinary glass bottle with a few layers of mutton cloth bound very tightly around it with sail twine. He explained to me when this chatti was filled with water and the mutton cloth soaked; the whole thing could be hung outside the porthole to catch the breeze. Even in a hot breeze, the water inside the insulated bottle would be quite cool within a couple of hours.

After teatime while I was doing the washing-up, the chief steward came into the pantry. He said he wanted to see me in his cabin when I'd finished, adding he wanted my signature for something and I could use his solid gold pen. When I later arrived at his cabin he had me sit down on his settee and gave me a bar of chocolate, I was absolutely dumbstruck and asked him what good deed I'd performed to deserve such a reward. Mr. Perkins looking at me with his beady little eyes then said in little more than a whisper, "Listen scouse, can you make a timber hitch?" I nodded as I was peeling the chocolate from its wrapper, then he said, "I want you to do a little job for me, it's a job that requires utmost secrecy and if I thought you had a big mouth I wouldn't ask you." I was quite flattered and asked him what the job was. He replied saying I must come back to his cabin at exactly twenty minutes past midnight, and most importantly I mustn't breathe a word to anybody or be seen arriving at his cabin. As I was leaving his cabin, – the chocolate having already been devoured, – he said, "There could be more chocolate on the way." I went down aft wondering how the chief steward knew what a timber hitch was and what lay in store. I strongly suspected I was required to take part in some illegal act.

While the long wait to midnight began, I made my first chatti using an empty fruit juice bottle with some mutton cloth I'd acquired from Big Ron. In the hot gentle breeze it was hung outside the cabin porthole until late evening. Then I found success with lovely cool, almost cold water. Just before twenty minutes past midnight I slipped up the after deck, past those who slept on the hatches, then up to the chief stewards cabin. It was a still moonless night lit only by the stars, the only noise was from the diesel engines thudding away and the water rushing past. I arrived at the cabin of Mr. Perkins which was lit only by his bunk light, he was awaiting my arrival. Next door to the chief steward's cabin was the third mate's, he'd just come off watch at midnight and whatever was going to happen had to wait until he'd got his head down.

Once more I sat down on the chief's settee while he gave instructions as to his requirements, and once more his voice was subdued to a whisper. "Now listen scouse I want you to go down number three hatch, on a heaving line, and send up six sacks of spuds from the 'tween deck on the starboard side." I nodded and told him I knew where the spuds where and it would be no problem. I asked him how he knew what a timber hitch was, to which he replied he had also once been on deck and had served for many years as a bosun.

The designated point of entry into the number three hold was in fact right outside on the deck, just a few feet away from the chief steward's cabin. There was slight movement and noise outside on the deck, where I could hear battens being slid out of the hatch cleats. The chief slipped quietly outside and through his doorway which was curtained off. I could hear him whispering to someone else before he came back in; a minute later he went out again and on his return whispered it was now time to go. He told me the corner hatch board had been removed, the heaving line was made fast to a ring bolt, and all I had to do was slide down the heaving line, send up the spuds and come straight back to his cabin.

I went outside on the deck where it was pitch dark and seemingly there was nobody around, however I knew somewhere in the shadows, there was somebody who was waiting to pull the spuds up. I slid the ten feet or so to the 'tween deck on the heaving line, it was pitch black, but I had my bearings. Soon after I'd brought the first fifty-six pound sack of spuds underneath the hatch opening. Then with the other end of the heaving line, I put a timber hitch around the sack and whispered up to the chief who was leaning over the hatch coaming. The fifty-six pound sack of spuds quickly went up, but I knew it wasn't the chief who was on the other end of the line as it went up at speed. I doubted if he could even lift one of those sacks off the deck, let alone pull it up and through the hatch coaming so fast.

The whole operation took just a few minutes, and as soon as I emerged on deck Mr. Perkins ushered me to his cabin. The reward for my sins was six bars of chocolate valued at 3/- and two bottles of fruit juice worth 6/8d, I was delighted. I had to sit down in the chief's cabin for a few more minutes until he gave me the all clear. While I was sitting there, I asked him in a whisper who pulled the spuds up, he looked at me puzzled and said he'd pulled them up himself; I told him I didn't believe him. I then said it was the first time in my life I'd ever done anything dishonest. It was the first time I'd ever heard anyone snigger in a whisper, but that's what Mr. Perkins was able to do; then he said the only thing God had forgotten when he made us all, was to make an honest Scouser.

After venturing out on deck again, Mr. Perkins told me to forget forever what had just happened. As I went out and past the hatch I'd just been down, I noticed it was now properly battened down again, with the tarpaulins tucked in the cleats, as well as the batten bars and wedges all neatly in place. By this time it was about 01h00. I walked around the poop housing noting the bosun who lived on the after end still had his lights on and hadn't turned in. I then went down to my cabin to discover Fred who seldom slept on deck, also hadn't turned in. Next morning before I turned to, and through the pantry porthole, I saw Fred driving home the wedges which had been removed six hours previously. At lunch hour I was to observe Fred walking aft with an object resembling a case of beer hidden beneath a piece of burlap. But of course, I didn't know what it was, and neither was I supposed to know who the shadowy figure or figures were who pulled the spuds up, then battened the hatch down again.

The engine was stopped for repairs on the second day out. There wasn't the slightest breath of wind and what had seemed unbearably hot, was now even more so. The temperature on deck was 120F and in the accommodation it was a lot higher, probably 140F; it was a place nobody went into unless they absolutely had to. At night most people slept on deck. In the daytime the steel decks were blisteringly hot, to walk on them without footwear was unthinkable. Everybody on the ship wore headgear and the bosun had told me whenever I was out on deck, even when going from aft to amidships, I had to wear a shirt and something to cover my head even if it was my dunce's hat from school.

I'd thought when the ship was in Port Sudan the water couldn't get any clearer, but here in the middle of the Red Sea with the ship stopped, and where the seabed was about five hundred feet deep, the rocks on the bottom could be seen. I emptied the gash bucket over the wall expecting loads of sharks to arrive on the scene, but there were no visitors; later on I threw in the silver lid from a tobacco tin. As it slowly sank catching the rays of the sun, it attracted a load of fish, but I didn't see it go right down to the bottom, and I suspected one of the fish ate it on the way.

We had cold salad at teatime, and after the floury old potatoes we'd had for the past few weeks, there were lovely new 'hatch' potatoes on the menu. Some of those in the mess room made favourable comment on this little delicacy which made me feel quite pleased. I didn't dare breathe a word where they'd come from and my eyes were focused on Fred and the bosun. I wanted to see what their reaction was to the comments; but they must have both been good actors, as their faces remained unmoved.

After four hours the engines were re-started and the ship continued towards Aden, soon land was visible on both sides of the ship. On the starboard side there was French Somaliland, whilst on the port, South Arabia. I was informed this narrow straight was referred to by seamen as 'The Gates of Hell' owing to its entry into the Red Sea. The general feeling is once we had passed through this straight heading southward, then the weather should become a little cooler. The ship arrived at Aden six hours later at midnight.

The Arabian Sea

Aden, August 18 1953. The ship was anchored and a huge bumboat looking like Noah's Ark which arrived at 04h00 was secured alongside. The local king of these bum boatmen was called Abdullah, and he – like George Roby of Port Said – was the one who seems to have the selling contract with the ships. The system of selling was so designed, crew members wishing to make purchases from his craft, could do so by first boarding his vessel; which was more like a floating warehouse and was crammed with just about everything imaginable. After selecting his purchases, the buyer then signed for them aboard his bum boat; the list was later taken on board the ship where the hard working chief steward paid the bum boatman in cash. The amount for the goods was then signed for again and deducted from the crewman's wages. Of course the chief steward didn't provide this service for nothing, and no doubt was given a percentage of all the transactions, as was the captain

Listening to the mess room talk, I was led to believe many chief stewards of ships had a reputation for playing the fiddle; and more often than not they worked in close harmony with the captain. In certain cases, these accusations may or may not be true, but their accusers spoke of chief stewards all living in large houses, being the owners of motor cars and living in the lap of luxury. Of the many perquisites open to the chief steward, the bumboat mentioned was just an occasional one. There was also the bond, where either the chief steward or the captain, or both, own its contents and could sell at any price they liked. Ten percent was the usual profit margin, and this could be quite a sum after a four or five month voyage. There was also subsistence money, where in some volatile countries and where the rate of exchange fluctuated wildly, the captain would delay giving a sub out until he could get the highest rate for sterling, then give it out to crew members at the lowest rate. Of all the sins the chief steward had the blame for, the most common was the one where he was accused of receiving backhanders in signing for food stores which never arrived on the ship.

As for the bumboat man, and unlike some of those people already mentioned in Port Said, Abdullah had a reputation for honesty, fair dealing, and was well spoken of. One point of note is Aden was completely duty free and anything bought there could be bought more cheaply, and legally, than anywhere in the world, at least this is what I'd been told. In comparison with the duty-free cigarettes on board which cost eight shillings a carton, they could be bought from Abdullah for seven shillings, and all after he'd made his profit.

Well at least there was a bit of a cool breeze at Aden. The *Willesden* as well as being re-fuelled, had already begun discharging the cargo of potatoes from Egypt, less six sacks of course. The shoreline was most uninviting, its hills completely without greenery resembling huge mounds of clay. Of the vessels at anchor with us, there was one a few hundreds yards away on the port side called the *Novelist* of T & J Harrisons, it had its stern towards us. The others were too far away to read their names, but one was a Sam boat covered in rust, there were also two Fort boats, and a P & O passenger ship.

We left Aden in the afternoon on passage to Colombo. Unfortunately for me, it was curry and rice for tea, but I wasn't alone in my distaste for the meal as Curly Megginson also had no liking for it, we had to be content with steam duff, bread and jam.

I'd previously seen a few flying fish in the Red Sea, but in the Arabian Sea there were a lot more and much bigger. As the ship pushed its way through the water, huge shoals of them would regularly take off. They would fly a hundred yards or more before dropping back into the water; I was told they drop back in when their wings become dry. The dolphins were in abundance too and I never tired of watching them (after working hours of course). One thing I was pleased about, was since I'd injured my hand in the fight with Ron Stafford, the bosun seemed to have forgotten all about the other three winch beds which were to be cleaned. Well if things worked out right and he forgot completely, I would remind him about them on pay off day. By now, I'd made half a dozen chatti's which were already hanging outside the mess in the starboard alleyway, it was always nice to see someone walk past and take a swig of cool water; although the weather was hot, it wasn't so bad as in the Red Sea.

To get my own back on the bosun for spoiling my afternoons by making me work, I began a nice little scheme. After he'd given me some job or other that would always be unpleasant or filthy, and if the job was on the after-deck, I'd do the vanishing trick. I'd disappear down the engine room escape hatch which came out in the recreation room, and once down in the propeller shaft tunnel I'd have a smoke for ten minutes or so. I told Ron Stafford about my ploy, and he joined me in the tunnel to light up. Things backfired though because while we were perched up on a ledge playing eye spy with my little eye, Old Albert came along the tunnel oiling the bearings as the shaft revolved. We had to wait without showing our presence until he'd gone back in the engine room again, I know if he'd caught me he'd have told the bosun.

From the time I'd descended the sixty-four rung ladder until going back up and getting back to work again, it must have been nearly half an hour. The bosun was irate demanding to know where I'd been. I told him I'd been to the toilet, but he screamed back at me saying he'd been in the toilets as well as having searched the ship high and low. He went on ranting he was just about to report me to the bridge as missing. Later on Bill Houston approached me; he asked me where I'd been for the half an hour I was adrift. I told him with a laugh I'd been down in the shaft tunnel where I could have a smoke in peace away from the swine of a bosun.

It was the first time I ever saw Bill lose his rag. He told me the bosun like everyone else had his job to do, and there was no wonder he was always onto me and I'd have to learn to pull my socks up. I got a real good lecture off him. He then told me about the importance of being a good shipmate, of how just trying to be friendly with everybody was only half the requirement. When I later went into the mess room I was mystified to find none of the sailors would talk to me. It later dawned on me word had gone around and none of them approved of my afternoon's actions. Although by now everybody knew of my private smoko in the shaft tunnel nobody told the bosun, but the message was clear. I never again did the vanishing trick.

I wasn't allowed in the saloon pantry on the second steward's orders, so during the next morning I was talking to Ron Stafford through the porthole. I was telling him of my previous day's folly, how nobody in the mess would talk to me as well as the cruel treatment I was always having from the bosun. Suddenly I heard the voice of the second steward, who unbeknown to me was in the saloon pantry. Having overheard what I'd said, he told me he'd been in the same position as me at one time, and had been given a dog's life from his second steward. He then told me to get his revenge, he'd put a teaspoonful of soojy soda in that second steward's tea resulting in him having the runs for three days. I had a strong feeling the second steward was trying to imply I poison the bosun with soda, but he wouldn't admit to it.

Later on during the afternoon, I was awe-stricken to see Captain Grist chipping and scraping the guard rails on the after end of the captain's deck. When he saw me peeping at him from out of the pantry porthole, he beckoned me to come forth. I don't know why, but just thought I was in for it for looking at him, however when I arrived on his deck all he asked me to do, was to go and get a chain stopper from Fred Hodges. I went to see Fred who was in the lamp room; I told him the Old Man of all people was chipping and scraping the rails and wanted a chain stopper. Fred didn't seem a bit surprised and said the captain was making up for all the work I didn't do. He gave me a chain stopper which was hanging under the focs'le head and I brought it to the Old Man. Captain Grist then asked me if I was surprised to see a captain chipping and scraping to which I replied I was. My first thoughts were he'd found out about my taking time off in the shaft tunnel and was trying to let me know by setting some kind of example. He asked me what would I be doing if I were the captain to which I replied I'd be having an afternoon sleep. He just gave a smile, then asked me how my previously injured hand was. After telling the captain my hand had made a full recovery, he told me to be careful when I had hold of a marlin spike, then he looked at me to let me know he didn't believe the marlin spike story.

The Old Man then wrapped the chain around the guard-rails and with a single round turn began pulling back and forth, the paint and rust just flew off.

It appeared Bill Houston and the rest of the crowd had by now forgiven or forgotten my previous day's misdemeanor, but it wasn't nice being sent to Coventry even if it was for only one day.

One good thing about the hot weather was I only ever had to wear a pair of shorts and flip-flops, then put a shirt on when I went on the wheel. Another was when I did my dhobying at night it only took a couple of minutes to do and dried in next to no time.

A few nights after leaving Aden, I did the first lookout for John Coyne who was also the second wheel man in the eight to twelve watch. I'd never have imagined there were so many shooting stars around the planet earth, but in the Arabian Sea and at night they can constantly be seen, even criss crossing each other. I mentioned this to the third mate later on when I was on the wheel, he said the only reason I couldn't see them over the Liverpool skies was because the atmosphere over that city was constantly black with smoke. Another phenonomen I witnessed in the area, was the sighting of a ship's mast head lights, for what may well appear to be a ship's lights on the horizon is not necessarily so. The same ship may be well over the horizon, fifty or sixty miles away and well out of normal visibility. According to what George Chell told me, the ship's masthead lights by some act of nature, somehow get refracted into the night skies then back down again to sea-level. The lights may from time to time go in and out of view by appearing and suddenly disappearing, then possibly an hour after the first sighting, the ship comes into full view.

On this subject I later made comment in the mess room where some of the old-timers who had been in the Russian convoys agreed with me. I was told when in those convoys way up north it was sometimes possible in day-light, to see a ship which was over the horizon; sometimes it may appear in the sky sailing upside down, an actual mirror effect of what was on the water.

On another occasion I was on the lookout there was no wind and the sea was as smooth as glass, but because of the extremely long ocean swell the ship was pitching wildly. The focs'le head on where I was standing, went down so far we were shipping water right over the fore deck. Next morning, the last lookout man in the four to eight watch, took a dozen flying fish down to the galley, they'd been caught amongst the winches and the steam pipe casings.

To the sailors who wanted it, were issued two beers a day at 18h00, the bosun's allowance was four; most of the sailors didn't drink at sea, besides, the beer was too warm. Those who didn't want their beer wouldn't draw it for anybody else even for cash payment. This was because they didn't want to see their bond bill climb, reducing the size of their pay-off. One evening just after beer issue, I was walking towards aft down the port side when I had to pass the bosun and his buddy Fred. The bosun was sitting on the bitts, whilst Fred was leaning against the guard-rails, and they were both drinking beer. The bosun was well aware I was always looking for bits of paper to draw on, and on seeing me, called me over saying he had a nice surprise for me. Naturally I was quite suspicious, especially after my recent admonish-ment for doing the disappearing act during working hours; he stood up, put his beer on one of the bitts, and had me sit on the other, then went into his cabin. He came back with half a dozen navigation charts under his arm, and with a big smile on his face, gave them to me saying only after much persuasion, he'd acquired them from the second mate. I thanked him for his generous effort and remarked they were excellent for drawing on the back of; just the thing I wanted. He said one day if I ever got to be good, I must draw him a nice picture of the *Willesden*. (The front cover has been dedicated to the late Sam Barter, bosun of the MV *Willesden*.)

Then the crunch came when the bosun asked me why I didn't draw my allowance of two beers a day. I told him I didn't like beer, I was too young to draw it, and I'd rather use my money for chocolate and fruit juice anyway. He told me the chief steward wouldn't refuse me because he always spoke well of me, the bosun said I could draw my two beers each day, give it to him and be paid in cash. He then told me at the end of the voyage he would give me five shillings as well. Now I knew why he'd gone to the trouble of getting the charts for me; but it made me think, if I were to draw the two beers a day and keep it in my locker, he'd be calling me sir in no time. The next evening I stood in line for my beer issue, but on reaching the head of the queue, and when the chief steward saw me, he said just one word: "Scram." This single word statement and the way he said it, meant in no uncertain terms I was not to be issued any beer, either on that or any other day. Later on, I told the bosun of my failure to draw the two beers a day, and immediately he was back to his old ways.

Although there was one good thing about big bad Sam, which was he sometimes supported me. One of the most annoying things for me as the peggy, and after having made a good start to the day's work, and possibly being ten or fifteen minutes ahead of schedule, was to have all the effort wasted because of the insidious second steward. There had been a time set by the second steward for the collection of the dry stores, and this was at 09h00 each day; if for some reason I wasn't there to collect on time, I would not get the stores. This absenteeism had happened previously when I was on the focs'le head tying up in Port Sudan, and also when I was once late through my own fault; fortunately at the time I had a surplus of stores and the loss wasn't missed. Quite often the second steward himself would be five or ten minutes late to issue the stores, and this of course, led to the losing of any advantage I'd gained in my time schedule; at the same time I knew he was being late on purpose.

One morning whilst on passage from Aden to Colombo, and at the appointed time, I went to the store room to collect the daily tea and sugar ration. As usual the second steward wasn't there, so after waiting ten minutes I went in search, and found him in the saloon pantry where I asked him for the daily stores. By this time he knew I was collecting 'rejuvenated' tea leaves in a sack. He also must have surmised, during the past couple of weeks, and due to the heat where tea and coffee had hardly been drunk, I had accumulated an amount of tea and sugar stores. He told me according to what he'd heard from one of the sailors, I had surplus stocks of tea and sugar and under such circumstances I wasn't entitled to any stores. However I knew he was just having a calculated guess, none of the sailors would have ever said such a thing to him. He then told me it was too hot to drink tea in this weather, and to come back when it was cooler; not being in the position to argue, I said OK and left.

The tight-fisted second steward must have thought he'd won a great victory by scrimping on the crowd's stores. But when I saw the bosun a few minutes later and told him of second steward's actions, he tore right through the galley and into the saloon pantry to confront the miserly company's man. If ever I wanted a wish to come true, it would have been those two knocked hell out of each other, each leaving the other for dead. My wish was not to be granted though, because the bosun came back to the mess a short time later with his eyes still blazing; he told me to get my ration tins and go down below to collect the day's stores. When I arrived at the storeroom the second steward was awaiting my arrival. Despite his carefully acquired suntan, his face had gone white and he was trembling. He was trying his best to have a laugh about the recent incident saying it was all a big joke, but his hands were shaking so much he couldn't weigh the rations out properly and I got a bit extra tea and sugar. I often wondered just what the bosun had said to the second steward, it must have been good, because he was never late again either.

Smoko was at 10h30 and whenever possible, I'd go and give the helmsman a ten minute relief so that he could also have his coffee break. If I couldn't do so, the alternative was I'd bring him a cup of coffee up to the wheel house. The routine for the helmsman was every half an hour during working hours, he would ring the time on the wheel house bell. I liked ringing the bell so I used to go up at 10h25 so I could do so; on hearing the bell which indicated it was 10h30, the bosun would knock the hands off for smoko. Each time I went up on the wheel at morning smoko, I always rang the bell a couple of minutes earlier than the proper time, by doing this, the sailors who were well aware of my activities, would get an extra couple of minutes from their work. The third mate who would be in the wheel house never paid any attention by checking the clock, and all was going well until the bosun caught me. I must have been strongly under his suspicion because one day, no sooner had I rang the five bells than he came charging into the wheel house, his eyes were glaring and he pointed to the clock asking me where I'd learned to tell the time.

John Coyne, Bill Houston and John Cunningham were all in the eight to twelve watch; they were known as the breakfast seven-bell men. One of my jobs was to wake them up at 07h20, which would give them plenty of time to get washed or showered, then have their breakfast before going on watch at 08h00. On being woken, John Cunningham always turned over for another couple of minutes and needed at least one more reminder. Bill always got out of his bunk without any second telling, John Coyne was also no problem getting up. John had a full set of dentures and used to put them in a glass of water while he slept. Before I woke him up I always looked at his glass to see his 'clappers' grinning at me, but if I was ever a minute or two late I imagined I could see them snarling at me.

I must admit after getting out of my bunk each morning, it often took me a long time to wake up properly. Sometimes I'd be walking around half asleep, and on one particular morning I'd forgotten to put those three on the shake. It was twenty minutes to eight when I suddenly realized my error, and made a dash aft to wake them up. John Coyne was absolutely livid. The first thing he ever done on waking up was to put his dentures in, or he couldn't be understood. Then he'd reach for his tin of Justmans and roll himself a cigarette, but now there wasn't time to have a roll, and as he had the first wheel he'd have to forsake his smoke. A torrent of insults rained down on me and the city of my birth; I received his full fury during which he told me the bosun was right in his opinion of me being a useless waste of time. In trying to appease him, I offered to take his place on the wheel until he'd had his breakfast and his smoke, but he wouldn't have it. If there was anything John liked it was a good moan, and this little incident would keep him content all day. At 20h00 I did the first lookout for John but it was all to no avail, there was to be no forgiveness.

Colombo

Derricks were topped, hatches stripped and the ship anchored at Colombo Roads on August 27; it was uncomfortably hot and clammy, and as soon as I drank any water the sweat just oozed out of me. While we were at anchor awaiting the pilot to take us in, I saw a ship of Ellermans named *City of Liverpool.* She was emitting loads of smoke from her funnel, and the greasers who were also watching said she was blowing tubes (whatever that may be). When Mick Bayes saw the ship he told me it was full of scousers and when both ships were inside, I should go on board to see if there were any books. But I'd been learning funnel markings for the past three months, and knew the Ellerman boat was like the *Malakand* and full of Indians. On our arrival at the inner harbour where the ship anchored, we were all given injections for yellow fever, this made my upper arm quite sore, nobody else seemed to have been affected though.

There were quite a number of ships at the anchorage, and amongst the British vessels were Clan Line, Ellermans, Harrisons, P & O, and Stricks, there were also two German, a Swede and a Dane – all were cargo ships. The port was extremely busy with dozens of barges offloading the ships at their anchorage, then being towed to the rather inadequate quayside.

For the past couple of weeks I'd been suffering with toothache and the chief steward who'd blamed the affliction on my eating too much chocolate, had put my name down to pay a visit to the dentist. On the day of arrival at Colombo, and being at anchor, number three boat was to be lowered, those wishing to see the dentist or doctor waited to go ashore. Curly Megginson was doing the peggying while I would be away from the ship, and I quietly hoped it would be all day. While being lowered the boat fall became fouled

Above: The *Empress of Scotland* in her early days as the *Empress of Japan*.
Note the bridge wing cabs.

Below: The *Empress of France*, formerly the *Duchess of Bedford* also on the Liverpool–Montreal run

The *Empress of Australia*, previously under the French flag as the *De Grasse*.
She was noted unfavourably by seamen who gave the advice: 'Keep off De Grasse'.

Above: The SS *Fire Queen* was owned by T&J Harrisons of Liverpool and was the nineteenth ship to pass through the Suez Canal. From an original oil painting by the author.

Below: Amidst the ice and snow on the decks of the *Willesden,* Sam Barter (nearest) and Fred Hodges make their way through the hatch beams strewn across the deck.

The four-masted barque *Lawhill* from an original oil painting by the author.

Above: The *City of Liverpool* shown here in Cape Town's Table Bay. She was at Colombo with us.

Below: This is the *Bradford City*. They beat us 3 – 0 in a football match.

The peggy

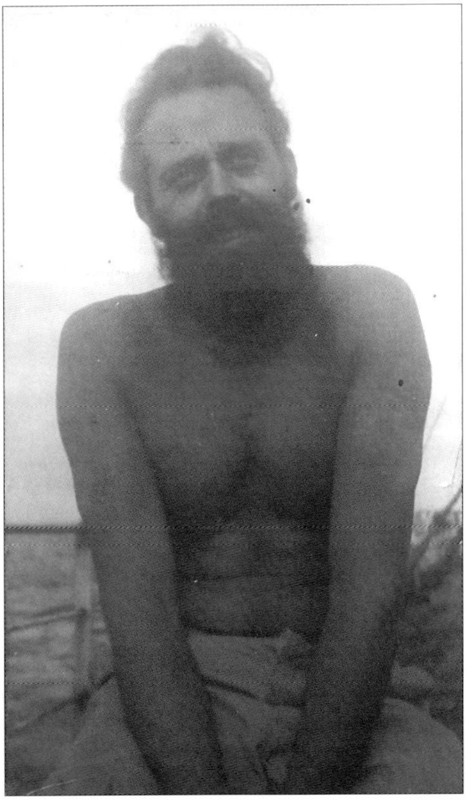

Left: Fred Hodges, my cabin mate

Right: The peggy, again.

HMS *Gambia*. She was at Port Said with us.

Athenic. Big Ron's last ship

SS *Norton*. Bill Houston's previous ship.

up on the stag horns and stranded. There was no way the fall could be extricated from its being jammed and we had to use the whole of the deck crowd and lots of Norwegian Steam to clear it. Eventually we got away and I had two back teeth filled at the dentist.

I found Colombo to be a most uninspiring place, unfortunately, and because the cargo handling was so primitive, we remained there until September 12. The main reason for the long stay, was some of the cargo destined for Madras had been discharged at Colombo. On the error being discovered, we went alongside for it to be loaded back on board again. I received a £2 sub, there were fifteen rupees to the pound and fourteen annas to a rupee.

During our stay I'd had been ashore a few times, and on one of those occasions I met up with two ratings from a British sloop. Their ship was at Trincomalee on the other side of the island, I just can't remember their ship's name, it was either the HMS *Wren*, or *Pelican*. They'd been out from the UK for over two years on the Far East Station. Unfortunately whilst homeward bound, where the ship was to be scrapped, one of their prop shafts had broken and they had to wait for a spare to be shipped out from the UK. They said by the time they paid off they'd have been out for over two and a half years, they looked pretty dejected.

In Colombo, the only thing I'd seen of any interest was in the market place; it was quite the thing there to see a stage show of a mongoose and a cobra fighting to he death. At the end of each fight (which the mongoose always won) the watching crowd would throw in a small donation for the owner of the snake; he would then have to acquire another cobra for the next show. I was convinced every single person in Colombo was dressed in white, they mostly wore shifts like an old man's nightshirt, and only the most affluent had shoes. Then there was the gilly-gilly man who had three little cups which he'd slide around upside down on his table. Under one of those cups was a small ball, and the challenge, after he'd moved them around, was for any onlooker to ascertain under which cup the ball lay. After he'd given Ron Stafford and me a little demonstration, he then asked me to identify the cup which hid the ball, and as he'd already planned in advance, I guessed right. He then asked Ron to do the same thing and he was also successful. The gilly-gilly man had a sharp pair of eyes which were full of craft and cunning, they reminded me of Mr. Perkins' – and the moneylender from South Shields. He suggested I have a little gamble to make the contest a little more interesting. I bet an Anna which is about the same value as a halfpenny and won, then I bet two Annas and won again, then five annas and won yet again! Ron was watching all this and was highly amused, because he knew what the plan was to be. The gilly-gilly man showing his exasperation, then told me I was far too clever for him but asked me wouldn't I like to bet a whole rupee on the outcome of the next forecast. The trap had been set but neither Ron nor myself was going to be caught in it. Much to the annoyance of the gilly-gilly man, Ron and I made off with our winnings – worth about threepence. Everywhere we went we were followed by hordes of beggars who were mostly children asking for 'backshees'. In trying and get rid of them, we jumped into a hand-pulled rickshaw telling its operator to go as fast as he could to the middle of town. The throng of beggars gave chase and easily kept up with the rickshaw and its rather frail operator; the streets and pavements were absolutely packed with people and there was no escape. Eventually I threw the winnings into the air where there was a wild scramble for it, but the chase of the beggars resumed, all the way back to the ship.

On Saturday afternoon the tattoo man came aboard and set up shop in the recreation room. I watched at first as some of the sailors had tattoos inscribed on their arms and shoulders; then Old Albert of all people took up the challenge. As some of the sailors were playing crib, drinking beer, or just watching the tattooist at work, Old Albert lay on his back for the 'artist' to work on him; he was going to have one right in the middle of his chest. The tattooist had a book full of pictures from which any prospective customer could take his pick, then have the one of his choice tattooed anywhere on his body he liked. Old Albert selected a picture of a partly dismasted sailing ship in a sinking condition going down by the stern; underneath was the inscription 'A Sailor's Grave'. The tattoo man first of all drew a preliminary picture in red ink on Albert's chest, then on finishing, showed him his drawing in reverse using a cracked mirror. After Old Albert had been satisfied with the initial drawing, the artist went to work. As the needle gouged out the tattoo, it could be heard quite clearly as it jarred his sternum bone, there was blood everywhere, but not a murmur from Old Albert. After the 'operation' which took nearly an hour, the blood was wiped off and the fee of five rupees was paid. Those who'd already been tattooed told me the needle was just a tingling sensation, and getting a tattoo didn't hurt at all. I was then encouraged by the sailors to have one on my arm and be like them, so after much persuasion I agreed. I'd selected a parrot and a snake on the branch of a tree and put my arm on the table for the 'artist' to work on, but was soon to discover the pain was excruciating! I was in agony and made my feelings known to the crowd of spectators who were in stitches laughing at my plight. After the tattoo man had worked on me for a few seconds I offered to pay his fee and cancel the job, but I was called a coward by the onlookers and reminded what ink had already been tattooed couldn't be withdrawn. For the rest of my life I'd have to go around with a bit of a tattoo on my arm, and my children and grandchildren and all who ever saw me would know I couldn't stand a bit of pain. Eventually the job was completed and I paid my two rupees; I just couldn't help wondering what pain Old Albert had gone through.

Another thing I'd been wondering about for the past couple of weeks, was where had all the new potatoes from number three hatch gone, they certainly hadn't gone into our mess.

John Levitt the cabin boy was in big trouble. On Saturday he was supposed to put the officers' suppers out but went ashore instead and was logged 10/-. On the following Tuesday Jim Dawson the assistant steward was also logged 10/- for being insolent to the mate in the saloon.

The Indian Coast

Nobody was sorry to leave Colombo; it wasn't such a nice place. The sea watches all changed one watch forward. This system of changes carried out on most merchant ships ensured everybody not only had a change of watch but also a change of mate on the bridge.

The heat and humidity was very high when we left the capital of Ceylon, so high in fact, the butter would melt in the dishes from solid to liquid within half an hour. For this reason the butter dishes were placed in the saloon pantry fridge when not in use.

One thing I couldn't understand with regards to the issue of food-stuffs, was why tea, sugar and condensed milk were so highly valued while butter, which cost a lot more, was freely available. In general and from what I'd heard the ship was a good feeder, but the persistence of this little bit of tea, sugar, and milk stinginess continued, apparently it was the done thing on most merchant ships.

At the after end of the mess room, the bosun sat on the same table as Achmid the chippy and Fred the lampy. On their previous voyage the bosun and Fred, as well as Captain Grist, had served together on another of Watts Watts's ships called the *Twickenham*. Frequently, everybody in the mess would hear the bosun say, "Hey Fred, remember the time on the *Twickenham*?" after which the bosun would go on about some incident or other which had taken place. This happened at nearly every meal time, and eventually, unknown to the bosun or Fred they became known to all in the mess as 'The *Twickenham* Twins'.

At one particular teatime the mess room was full except for the bosun and Fred. I was under the impression they were aft drinking their beer issue as was often the case. I walked out of the pantry into the mess room where everybody was seated, then just to create a bit of humour I said for all to hear, "Hey Fred remember the time when we were on the *Twickenham*?" I expected everyone to have a laugh, but instead there was a stoney silence. Suddenly from behind the bosun bellowed, "What are you talking about? You were never on the *Twickenham*." My face must have gone white with fear. Later on when the bosun had eaten and left the mess room, there was an uproar of laughter while I was still recovering from my fright. The bosun hadn't twigged on to my sarcasm, but I knew if it'd been Fred who'd come from behind instead of the bosun, he wouldn't have been fooled. Fred didn't usually say much but I knew he'd have just looked at me with his steely eyes which in a way was often worse than the bosun's roaring.

The tattoo I'd had done in Colombo gave me a bad time and went septic, I showed it to the chief steward who put iodine on it. After a couple of days the scabs went away but it itched a lot. Mr. Perkins told me the tattooist had no doubt been using the same needle on all his customers for a long time, and if any of his previous customers 'had anything' then I was liable to touch out for whatever they had; he showed me his fat little arms indicating he didn't believe in such rubbish as tattoos.

One teatime on passage to Madras, I really upset the bosun with the most minor of offences. The 'crime' was I'd placed a half a pound block of butter in his butter dish without taking the wrapper off. He started bawling at me for committing this terrible offence then picked up a sauce bottle which hadn't had its top wiped clean. The admonishment intensified for the sake of those in the mess and in which he stated I was the most useless peggy he'd ever seen, further to which I was a 'menace to shipping!' This brought giggles from all in the mess, Paddy Dolan couldn't stop laughing and his mouthful of food went all over the deck; the bosun glared at Paddy as if to ask, was he laughing at the peggy or him. After this little incident I was quite often called a 'menace to shipping' by the sailors.

On arrival day at Madras I was to help in the topping of the derricks on the fore deck. As the derrick head lashings were being released and the guys being set, the bosun told me to go down below and ask for steam on deck. I'd never had the opportunity of topping the derricks before and as it was something new to me, I wanted to make sure I didn't miss out on anything. I ran from the fore deck to the top of the engine room, then just as I was about to descend the long set of ladders to the starting platform, I saw Old George on the middle deck. Amidst the noise of the big diesel engine I shouted to George to give the bosun steam on deck. Old George waved back and I felt happy I didn't have to go all the way down below. Now I could get back on deck, where with a bit of luck, and if the bosun wasn't around, I might havea go at driving the winch.

I raced back to the fore deck telling the bosun steam was on its way. By now everything was ready for the derricks to go up, and everyone waited for the tell-tale sign of the cracking noise of steam coming through the pipes. We waited and waited but still no steam, then after ten minutes or so, the impatient bosun glared at me and asked who I'd seen for the steam on deck. I replied telling him it was Old George. As though he didn't believe me, he sent John Dick down below to ask for steam on deck. We didn't have to wait long, for even before John had returned, the cracking in the pipes told us steam was on its way; the derricks then started going up and that was that, or so I thought.

On our way towards number three and four hatches amidships, the irate bosun called me over. He had his hands on his hips, his eyes glaring and he roared at me saying he'd just spoken to Old George, who'd told him nobody had asked him for steam on deck. I just couldn't believe it, I didn't dare answer the bosun back or even try to explain what had happened, so I was well and truly in the dog's box. Later on I approached Old George telling him of the trouble I'd been in, I asked why he hadn't supplied the steam on deck when I shouted down for it. He thought for a moment, then asked me, "Is that what you wanted when you was at the engine room top?" He then told me in such circumstances when someone shouts to him in such a manner he just waves back. He said he didn't know I wanted steam, how was he supposed to hear me above all the engine room noise. He said next time I wanted something like steam, I must come below and tell him properly.

When we got to Madras the first thing to happen was the whole ship's company had injections for cholera. We were told because of the powerful serum, the injection was to be administered in two parts, one half today, and the other tomorrow. The first part of the jab was administered and I thought nothing unusual about it, but when the time came for the second part the following day, my left arm where I'd had the first jab had gone terribly stiff and painful. Therefore I had the other jab in the right arm and within a few hours both arms had seized up. But stiff or not, there was no let up in the work. It was just as well I wasn't looking for sympathy with my two arms in agony, because it's one thing never found on ships. Apparently, and from what I was told, nobody else was much affected by the cholera jab because of their relative size and weight, and in my case it should have been spread over four days.

Number three hatch was stripped and the bosun gave me the job of pumping up the tyres on the captain's car. The foot-pump proved pretty useless and I suspected the leather washer inside it was well worn, however I was glad, with my arms in such pain, it wasn't a hand-pump. Eventually it took me about half an hour to pump up the two front tyres by which time I was exhausted with the heat of the 'tween deck. Tug and Gilly then came down to take the lashings off the car, and seeing me in my state of near exhaustion pumped up the other two tyres for me, the car was then landed on the quayside.

After Captain Grist had driven off in his motor car, I wondered why I couldn't have pumped the tyres up on the quayside, it wasn't as hot there as it was in the 'tween deck. I didn't ask why though, and thought the bosun was punishing me for something I may have done. At teatime I was pumping water to the galley with my stiff arms when the bosun came up. He glared at me first, then gave me a five rupee note, he told me it was a backhander from Captain Grist for pumping his tyres up. The bosun said I didn't deserve it and if it had been Captain Barter instead of Captain Grist then I'd get nothing, I was dying to tell him it was Tug and Gilly who'd done the job. Maybe I would wait until paying off day before breaking the news.

In the evening some of the crowd and myself went ashore to watch a film show. It was a cowboy film and despite the audience being adult, a chorus of cheers greeted every heroic deed by the 'goodies'. At the end of the film in which the goodies proved victorious in killing all the baddies, everyone stood up and applauded wildly. There were two of the sailors who never accompanied us to the cinema, they'd gone bagging off instead; at breakfast time next morning we were all to hear of the adventures of the two Romeos.

One of them said at dusk, and after he'd paid for the services of a 'business lady' he'd selected, her 'agent' escorted him to a bamboo hut, which was illuminated by a single candle. As he was lying on a straw mat awaiting his partner's arrival, he thought he saw the wall of the bamboo shack move. Later on, when his eyes became accustomed to the weak candlelight, he discovered it wasn't the wall which was moving, but it was alive with huge cockroaches known as Bombay tigers. The great lover who was known by all on board to have a phobia for these insects, never bothered waiting for the promised favours or for a return of the fee, but grabbing his clothes ran naked out of the shack. As for the other Romeo, he'd decided on being allocated a partner of unsuitable facial appearance, he took the option of abstaining, and so they both came back to the ship empty-handed.

Paddy Dolan bought a mongoose for a pet. One would never think this tame little creature, resembling a ferret, could be such a killer when faced with a snake. He kept the mongoose in his cabin with the intention of bringing it back to the UK, but in the mess they all said it would die long before it got there. One of Paddy's plans for the animal was to let it loose down the holds when the ship was light. Beneath the limber boards there would be plenty of rats in the bilges for it to amuse and feed itself. There were also plenty of jaspers living and breeding behind the hot press in the pantry, those little brown things are called cockroaches or steam flies by some people. I would regularly spray behind the hot press with insecticide, but it appeared that the jaspers thrived on it. According to the experts in the mess the only way to be rid of them is by constant fumigation. It was a waste of time fumigating just once then going away when they all appear to be dead; the fumigation must be carried out at five day intervals to kill the newly-borns before they had a chance to breed again.

While we were in the port, someone from the *Bradford City* a ship belonging to Smith's of Cardiff, came around and challenged us to a game of football. The *Bradford City* had been out for eighteen months and had developed a good football team; we played in the evening and lost 3-0.

To me there didn't appear to be any difference between Colombo or Madras with regards to the people or the customs. Rickshaws were plentiful as were the hordes of beggar children who packed the streets. The smell of curry was everywhere – just like Colombo, I didn't enjoy my stay in Madras.

During the afternoon I saw the chief steward leaning over the bulwarks and stopped to pay my respects. I asked him did he want any more little jobs done. "Little jobs?" he inquired. "What kind of little jobs?" I reminded him of the sacks of spuds which had been purloined whilst the ship was in the Red Sea. The chief steward was an excellent actor and pretended he knew nothing about any spuds in the Red Sea. He told me if I wasn't careful I'd get into serious trouble talking like that. Mr. Perkins was more than a little annoyed, and I felt a bit foolish.

Calcutta

After a four-day stop we sailed for Calcutta, arriving at the mouth of the River Hoogly at 16h00 on September 20, it was too late to go up the river and we anchored until the next morning. After teatime the crowd were all aft and I saw sharks for the first time, not one, but a dozen or so swimming in the muddy brown water around the stern. They weren't the big ones I'd heard about, and were probably six feet in length. I had the gash bucket on the rail and was about to empty it in, when instead, I threw an empty sauce bottle into the water. As it floated a shark came up and bit it swallowing half of it, then before the other half had a chance to sink it swallowed that too. When the bucket was emptied into the water, there was such a frenzy as the sharks fought for the slops, one would think the propeller was going full ahead.

Next morning September 23, anchor was weighed at first light, the ship then proceeded up river towards Calcutta. We passed loads of little canoes with a lone fisherman aboard each of them, there were dozens of craft which I think were houseboats, and even on the river banks there were multitudes of people. The ship arrived off the Kiddipore dock in the afternoon, but every berth in the dock was occupied. It later transpired there had been a bit of mistiming amongst the authorities, a City boat which was supposed to have sailed in the afternoon had been delayed, and now there was no berth available for the *Willesden.* The ships which were in the dock were locked in and were safe, but any ships in the river had to take defensive action against the elements.

In the River Hoogley there's a bore wave which rushes up the river at certain times. I never found out if this was just seasonal or permanent, however the way things turned out, our ship had to go alongside in the river berth then take the force of this bore wave. First of all the ship tied up starboard side to, then the starboard anchor was landed on the jetty. Using a large labour force of locals, the anchor was knocked and broke at the first joining shackle. Then the cable was paid out along the quay; part of it was broke and used to secure the ship aft, the rest of it was hauled in by the windlass. It was quite a lengthy process of securing alongside, and according to the sailors most unusual, although one of them said it was a procedure he'd recently performed in some other port he'd visited in the Pacific.

At about 19h00 the ship was secured alongside with the anchor cables. All the bitts were full and every headspring, backsprings and berthing rope was out doubled up and with slack on them. It was going dark by now and all the cluster lights were on all over the ship, everybody was on stations and even the river pilot was on board just in case the ship broke free. I was on the focs'le head at the time the bore was seen to be coming up river, and when it got closer to us, it appeared to be no more than six feet high. Thinking back to the forty and fifty-feet waves we'd seen in the Atlantic, I laughed a bit at this little wave of six feet. Then it hit us from aft! The stern lifted up and the ship ranged forward quite fast. The anchor cable, which came out of the hawse pipe and led aft carried away. One or two of the stern lines and springs also went, but otherwise there was no damage done. We then resumed securing alongside, finishing at 22h30, probably the person who had the most to do in the whole operation was Achmid the chippy. Next morning the City boat sailed, so after the starboard anchor had been re-assembled and shipped, we took the vacant berth inside the dock. It now meant we wouldn't have to tie up with the anchor cables again. Once we were alongside the cargo started coming out.

If I'd thought there were a lot of people in Colombo or Madras I soon realised there were an awful lot more in Calcutta. The place was absolutely crammed. On every street corner, in every shop doorway, and everywhere I went there was a beggar; on Calcutta Bridge there were hundreds of them. Many were deformed and I was led to believe in a lot of cases, these deformities were administered by the parents of the beggar at childhood, thus enabling the child to have a more profitable future begging.

After tea time we played football with some ship from the Stag Line, I can't remember her name but I think it was a Fort boat. They'd been out for twenty-one months running constantly with a steel cargo between Australia and Calcutta. I spoke to some of the crowd who said they'd had a rotten trip, their ship was really hungry and many of their crowd had skinned out in Australia, but now – at last – they were homeward bound. The peggy who'd signed on as first trip deck boy was now SOS and said he was going in for his EDH ticket when the ship paid off in a couple of months time. We had a bit of a job getting a football team up on our ship; we had a lot of old men on board and two from their ship had to play for us. The football match went OK although the heat was sweltering and we were beaten 3-1, Mr. Collister our third mate scoring the goal for us.

For lunch time sweet on the next day, Peter Kingham the second cook had made the most delicious looking jam tart I'd ever seen. After carefully assessing there'd be plenty of leftovers, I did without my plateful of dinner, thereby ensuring there would be enough room in my belly for the tart. After having washed up, I took a large enough chunk of the leftovers to make up for the dinner I'd forsaken. I was thinking how nice it was going to taste as I made my way down aft where a few of the sailors were sitting on number six hatch waiting to be turned to. I held the tart waist high in both hands when, 'whoosh' it disappeared from my hands. The thief was one of those big black buzzard birds which abound in the city of Calcutta; the locals regard these carrions as some kind of sacred bird, because they eat all the dead bodies which are cast adrift on the river. Well if curses work the buzzard who stole my tart died in agony within a minute, the air was blue and those who sat on number six hatch, who'd seen the bird make the snatch were highly amused. To try and get some revenge, I put a crust of bread on the corner of number six hatch and hid behind the winch, waiting unsuccessfully to maim one of them with a broom handle, the birds must have read my mind.

The people in Calcutta were incredibly poor. One of the hatch workers, who could speak English, told me his wages were two rupees, which was about three shillings for a twelve hour shift. The wages and port charges were so low, the ship worked right through each day and night of our stay. Some of the hatch workers slept in the 'tween deck when their twelve hour shift was up. They had no home.

The tailor came aboard and I was sized up for a quite stylish white shirt and a pair of shorts to match. The quality of the material was really good and a number of the crew had made to measure suits from the tailor. I was measured up at lunch time and at tea time, five hours later, the job was delivered. It was a perfect fit and the cost was five rupees, or seven shillings.

Lots of people seeking work came aboard to offer their services, dhobying, hair cutting, nail manicures, clothes ironing, and lots of other things. None of them as far as I could gather could read or write, but they all had letters of recommendation from sailors of mostly British ships. The letters made the most hilarious reading, most of their contents could never be repeated in these pages, but for example one would say: 'This lazy ..... has worked for me today, he is ...... useless and can't do anything properly.' Another applicant had a letter signed by a Doctor Ross of the Liverpool Seamen's Dispensary. Out of twenty or more job applicants who approached me, all their letters were headed by the ship on which they'd worked, and all were filled with the vilest wording about their holders' capabilities. Any job seeker on being turned down for employment would always ask for a reference, and of course I took great pleasure in writing a few of them out on the same lines as those I'd already seen. I gave one of them a job scrubbing out and soojying the alleyways, then polishing all the brass work, he was quite prepared to work hard for just a small payment. 'Shipshape and Bristol fashion' then came on the scene, I thought he was going to chase my labourer away and make me do my own work, but instead, he told me the labourer was a much better worker than me so he'd leave things as they were. For working all afternoon I gave him a rupee, some food and an honest well-worded reference, he was delighted.

The tattoo man came aboard later on, he had an electric needle which seemed much more sophisticated than the one used in Colombo where the 'artist' had used a kind of treddle machine. I now decided despite the pain I'd have to match the one on my left arm and had a swallow on my right forearm. It was a much better job and didn't hurt so much. I was determined to ensure this one didn't go septic. While the cargo was being discharged, other cargo was being loaded in the 'tween decks, this was jute and sacks of beans of some description and was probably going to the UK.

I didn't like Calcutta, everywhere I went there was sitar music and the smell of curry permeated the air. There were flies in the clammy heat of the daytime and mosquitoes in the even more clammy heat of the night. Ever since we'd been on the coast I'd suffered with mosquito bites, it was my ankles and wrists they seemed to like best. None of the applications the chief steward gave me worked. Fred Hodges didn't have any bites on him and when I asked him what his secret remedy was, he said there was no secret about it. He told me the mosquito's liked rotten meat and that's why they went for me – as he was nice and fresh they never bit him.

On the second night there, I saw a group of down and outs in the town smoking marijuana. I'd heard of this dope and been warned never to touch the stuff, but they wanted to sell me some. Judging by the appearance of the unfortunates, I thought the advice I'd previously been given on not touching it was correct. They were at the same time chewing beetle nut, this gave the appearance or impression they'd received a punch in the mouth and their teeth were bleeding. I didn't like Ceylon or India. Although nobody enjoyed the heat and humidity, I was unable to stand it as well as most of the others. I constantly felt worn out and looked forward to the time when we'd be back in the cold weather.

On Sept 28, we left Calcutta for Chittagong in East Pakistan. The ship was nearly empty and the old familiar vibrations and the crackling of the propeller came back. By now I was used to it and was more bothered by the night-time heat. At times I just dropped off to sleep with sheer exhaustion and each morning I would awake to find that the mosquito's had been having a good feed off me.

Even at sea it seemed to be just as hot, I couldn't understand how the two cooks in the galley could stand the added heat of the coal burning range. During the passage to Chittagong I was leaning over the galley half door having a talk with the cooks Big Ron and Peter, I was remarking on the humidity adding they both deserved medals. At the time Big Ron was preparing the lunch time meal making soup in a ten-gallon kit. As he leaned over the galley range with the sweat pouring off him, I couldn't help noticing a deluge of his sweat would find its way into the soup. I declined soup at lunch time.

Three days later on October 1, the ship arrived at Chittagong in East Pakistan. It was just a rickety wooden jetty we were secured to, and it was full of starving rabid dogs. Some had little or no fur and one or two of them were frothing at the mouth, which reminded me of the bosun. The notice on the gangway said simply 'No Shore Leave', and I was told not to go on the quay to empty the gash bucket for fear of being bitten by the dogs. After breakfast instead of going aft to empty the gash bucket I emptied it from the ship's side and onto the jetty. There was an almighty scramble for the slops as the wretched animals fought for it.

After working hours there wasn't really much for the crowd to do, so in the evening a crib tournament was organised; the prize was to be a bottle of beer. I wasn't in the competition because I couldn't play the game but I enjoyed watching as there were lots of exciting arguments going on. This was because of all the cheating and 'timber carrying' – the best cheat would win. Out of the sixteen contestants Big Ron the ship's cook won the tournament, he was the best undiscovered cheat on the ship. Apparently he gave the other finalist Gilly Smith a double skunk whatever that is, and it was the beaten finalist who was supposed to give the winner the bottle of beer. This never came about, because on seeing he was about to be beaten, Gilly quickly drank the last of his two beer issue.

There was a table tennis room on the starboard side, and sometimes I would play with the cabin boys. The stewards were the only ones who ever played table tennis, the sailors or the greasers never did. I was a bit annoyed about this because I was the one who had to scrub the compartment out. Therefore I used to lock the place up when clean, and then when the second steward wanted to play I'd make him wait until I was ready to unlock the door.

Homeward Bound Again

Maybe I hadn't been to many places in my life, but of those I had, Chittagong was by far the worst, and like everybody else I was glad to get away. As we let go and pulled in the last headline, the ship shuddered as her engines started up. Bill Houston then gave three cheers and shook hands with everybody on the focs'le. I was a bit confused by his actions and asked him what was the occasion. "Scouse," he replied, "We're now homeward bound." I always had a feeling Bill was well informed, and especially regarding the practicalities of shipping. He certainly seemed to know all about sailing ships, and often came up with some strange nautical terms and customs; the handshaking incident on the focs'le was just one of them. Later on I told Old George about this, and he said in the days of sail it was the done thing when any ship began her homeward bound run to give three cheers. He also told me in those days the average voyage of a deep-sea trip was two years.

Our next port of call was Vizagapatnam, where we were due to load a full cargo of manganese ore. Then the ports we were to visit on the homeward run were, Colombo, Aden, Suez, London, Antwerp, Hamburg, Hull, finally paying off at Middlesborough somewhere in the month of December.

Next morning, I went down to the freezer room to get some bread from Big Ron who'd won the crib tournament. He laughed as he told me that in order to win, he'd cheated in every game by carrying timber and in the final game a whole street of it. He said he didn't care about not getting the beer, only claiming the glory of winning. While I was down in the freezer he told me I looked as though I'd put on a lot of weight since we'd left Hull, and it was probably due to his irresistible *cordon bleau* cooking. I told him when

I'd joined the ship in May, I weighed eight stone fully-clothed but felt as though I'd put on weight. He then had me hold myself onto, and put my full weight on the hook of his meat scale, imagine my surprise when I found I weighed nine stone. I felt quite pleased about having put on fourteen pounds in eighteen weeks, I also thought if I was still in the sea school I'd probably have put one pound on. When we got into the mess big Ron thumped his chest, and told everyone about my one stone gain in weight, the bosun was the first to comment saying with all the food I'd eaten combined with the tiny amount of work I'd done, it should be two stone.

In the evening it was just going dark and we were all sitting on number six hatch talking, when suddenly morse signalling could be seen coming from out of the gathering gloom. It came from a ship on the starboard side, and the vessel didn't have any navigation lights showing. Mick Bayes who'd been in the Royal Navy as a communications rating read the message, he told us it was a British warship asking for identification. When he was asked what the name of the warship was, he said in such circumstances they never gave their name, only identifying them selves as one of HM ships.

By now and thanks to Paddy Dolan's mongoose, there wasn't one single cockroach in the crew pantry, yet despite being sprayed daily with insecticide the saloon pantry was as infested as ours had been. The mongoose unknown to the bosun had been named Sam, and for a few nights Sam was let loose in the saloon pantry; by the time we got to Vizagapatam the results were the same, not one jasper to be seen, Sam had caught and ate the lot.

On our arrival at Vizagapatnam on October 10, the chippy began building shifting boards. These weren't the same as the ones he'd made in Montreal used for loading grain, instead it was a kind of box he'd built on the ceiling of each hold. Meanwhile, a lifeboat had been lowered for painting the ship's side; John Dick and John Cunningham began painting the boot topping; the stages stowed on the poop housing were rigged, and soon most of the crowd were busy with brushes painting the ship's side. After lunch I was employed on the focs'le head with Curly Megginson and Paddy Dolan, we were to chip the paint and rust off the guard rails and give them a coat of red lead. Paddy went and got a chain stopper and cleaned the rails off just as Captain Grist had done a month earlier. Later on I busied myself sweeping up all the chippings, then after filling a bucket of them, emptied them off the focs'le head and into the water. I watched in fascination as the white chippings slowly sank, the sunlight reflecting on them made a dazzling sight. As I was leaning entranced on the rail I heard a bellow from behind. It was the bosun, and he wished to know the name of my daddy's yacht. I then received my daily admonishment. When he'd gone again Paddy and John had a good laugh at me, it so happened just for once I'd worked non-stop for an hour, then when I'd stopped for a few seconds I'd been caught. Paddy and John, who had spent much of their time lounging around and smoking had seen the bosun coming and, unable to warn me, had picked up their chipping hammers and went through the motions.

In the recent past I'd occasionally been reminded of the two boatmen from the Suez Canal who would be awaiting the arrival of the ship – and for me in particular. Now the reminders were daily, and prophesies were made as to my future as well as the type of death I was to suffer. Of all the ports we'd been to Vizagapatam appeared to be the best; there didn't seem to be so many beggars, although there were hundreds of rickshaws begging for business.

The loading of the iron ore was from a single shute and the ship had to be shifted from time to time. This allowed for the even distribution of the iron ore into the holds. Picking a piece up I found it was almost as heavy as lead. The cargo was loaded into the shifting board boxes on the ceiling and within a couple of days the ship was down on her marks. It was this short stay in port which provided the last opportunity to finish painting the ship's side and frantic efforts were made to complete the job. From the quayside, the ship looked very clean with her new coat of paint although by now the red boot topping was under water.

The ship was still in port on October 11 which being a Sunday meant a day's leave had been missed. The good thing about it for the deck crowd was they all had the day off, but for some strange reason I was the only one who had to turn to. At 11h00 there was to be captain's rounds and it turned out to be one of those days when everything went wrong for me. First of all, the crowd continued lounging around talking about their beloved city of 'Ull' in the mess; this didn't allow me to put the chairs up and scrub the place out. Then when I had completed the mess room and went aft to do the bathrooms and recreation room, I was about twenty minutes behind time. It was always easier doing the bathroom on rounds day though, because all the dhobi buckets were emptied and taken away by their owners. I could never understand why people want to leave all their gear soaking in a bucket when it's easier to wash it straight away. As soon as I'd finished I made for the recreation room, I knew the compartment was full of beer bottles and dirty ashtrays as well as the tables and deck which wanted scrubbing. It was 10h20 by then and I was late, but I knew I could have the whole place finished before the rounds party arrived at about 10h40 if I moved at speed. However, the bosun came along just as I was about to start; he told me I must go amidships and be in the messroom when the captain arrived. I tried to tell the bosun I had the recreation room to do, but it was like talking to a brick wall and off he went amidships.

Most of the deck and engine crowd were hanging around the after end of the ship, either sitting on the bitts or leaning against the guard rails having a lovely time talking and telling jokes about women. They jeered and warned me of the trouble I'd be in when the rounds party came for inspection; of the mate's face when he walked in the recreation room. I was to be logged, sacked, given a double DR, discharged and locked up in Vizagapatnam as a 'menace to shipping'. The bosun had by this time gone to join the rounds party and it was a good job he had after some of the choice names I'd called him. The air was blue and those who had the day off said they were going to tell the bosun what I'd called him behind his back.

I went amidships, a bag of nerves, to stand by the messroom and pantry not feeling at all happy. The rounds party had first inspected all the other parts of the 'midship accommodation then arrived in the messroom before going through their little ritual. I knew by now, I'd never have time to get aft and do the recreation room, and all because of those rotten swines from 'Ull' who could relax and enjoy the day off. As it would be a waste of time trying to explain or make excuses, I'd just have to face the wrath of the captain via the first mate and via the bosun, when they were confronted by the state of the recreation room.

When the inspection of the messroom and pantry was over, the bosun indicated I join in at the rear of the rounds party and as there was only the after accommodation left for the captain to see I tagged on. That today of all days I should have to accompany the rounds party was just too unfortunate. I couldn't say nor do anything, my opinion would not be sought on any matter, and the tension was mounting. By this time it was about 11h20 and going aft, the procession of inspectors visited all the accommodation leaving the recreation room until the very last. The deck and engine crowd who had previously been languishing around the after end had all disappeared; my heart was beating fast and I had a sense of great foreboding. As usual the mate opened the recreation room door and went in first followed by the captain. Then the rest of the entourage – looking like a procession of lepers – followed. All I could do was stand in the alleyway and await my fate. After a couple of minutes they started coming out, as usual the captain first. I was looking down at the deck waiting for it, when I heard Captain Grist say, "Well done peggy." I didn't know what he meant and assumed it was because he was such a gentleman he wasn't going to lay into me in front of everyone. The rounds party went away and I got my cleaning gear ready to attack the recreation room. What a shock I had when I opened the door, the place was absolutely sparkling, glistening, and spotless, and the crowd who had returned were in stitches laughing at me. I'd been set up, good style so I took back all the insults and curses I'd put on them and their city of ''Ull on't River 'Umber'.

Return to Colombo

Leaving Vizagapatam on October 12, we were bound for Colombo where some cargo had to be loaded, while cargo taken on at Calcutta was to be discharged. By now the ship was fully loaded and once again the vibrations had ceased just like when we'd left Montreal or London. When we arrived at Colombo the ship went alongside, and I was given a job which made cleaning under the winch beds look like child's play. The fresh water tank in number four 'tween decks had to be scaled from the inside before it was to be painted with lime. There was a manhole about fourteen inches in diameter which allowed access into the tank, according to the bosun I'd been carefully selected for the task because of my size. After the tank had been pumped out, the chippy took the bolts off and removed the manhole plate from the tank. A lead light was inserted and I was told to enter the tank which was about ten feet square and eight feet high – it absolutely stunk. Worse! there was about three inches of filthy brown water which hadn't been pumped out, and all the insides of the tank were covered with a brown slime; to think, this was where the drinking water for the whole ship had come from. Up on deck the weather was hot and humid, down in the 'tween deck the air was stifling, inside the tank it was all of that and more! John Dick who was also of small stature, was sent to accompany me on the task. Outside the tank there was Paddy who sent up the buckets of slime to the deck, then somebody had the relatively easy task of emptying the slime over the wall. John and I took it in turns to have a breather outside in the 'tween deck which by comparison now seemed cool. We scraped most of the day during which time Achmid the chippy had prepared a mixture of lime. We then had to paint the inside of the tank with this whitewash and wait for it to dry. I don't know how the chippy made it dry, he must have put an extraction fan in and left it on all night, because the next afternoon it was dry and I had to go back in and give it another coat. After the job was completed I asked the chippy when was the last time the tank had been cleaned. He said he didn't know but guessed at three or four years, maybe longer. The ship was nine years old and he said it was quite possible it had never been cleaned from new.

The ship was working cargo right through the night. Jim Dawson and Ron Gascoigne went ashore for a drink, and as there are no pubs or bars in Colombo, I assumed they'd gone on board another ship. Just before midnight when they arrived back on board, there was some trouble which eventually lead to a fracas. It appeared some incident occurred on the deck which led to an argument between Jim Dawson and Mr. Kirby the chief officer. In the heated discussion which followed, Jim Dawson was alleged to have pushed the mate. The third mate who was at that time supervising the cargo at number three hatch attempted to mediate and was given a shove by Ron Gascoigne. On hearing the commotion Captain Grist came out on deck where Jim Dawson swore at him. The police were called and came on board to keep the peace.

The next morning they were on the captain's carpet. Jim Dawson was logged £1 for insolence (this being his second offence) and for assaulting the mate he was logged 10/- making 30/- total. Big Ron was logged 10/- for being insolent to the captain, and a further 10/- for assaulting the third mate. Later on Jim told me the captain was going to press charges against him and Big Ron on the ship's arrival in the UK. He also told me he feared they were both to receive a DR for conduct.

It had previously been explained to me the meaning of a DR. In a seaman's discharge book there are two columns for recording his conduct and ability. This record follows him throughout his career, and may be the first thing any prospective captain or mate will want to look at before engaging him on his ship. In normal circumstances every seaman is given a 'Very Good' discharge in the appropriate columns of his discharge book. But if during a voyage some misdemeanor occurs, the likes of which Ron Gascoigne and Jim Dawson were involved, then their discharge may well record 'Good'. This discharge of 'Good' may sound fine to people who don't understand, but to those who do, it is a huge slur on the seaman's record of discharges. When any seaman has committed a serious breach of conduct and his captain thinks that even a 'Good' does not reflect the true character of the offender, then he may enter 'Decline to Report' for one or even both columns. This discharge is known as a DR and any person receiving one will have great difficulty in getting any kind of a ship in the future.

Curly Megginson who had been complaining of stomach cramps went ashore to see the doctor. On his return the news he brought was he was to be paid off. The bosun wasn't very pleased because he would now be a man short on deck, and with the ship homeward bound, every man was needed to spruce the ship up. After having a discussion with the mate, the bosun informed me I was to replace Curly in the eight to twelve watch; this meant I was to join up with Tug and Gilly. I was then told to carry on with the peggy's job in the forenoon watch, during which time Tug and Gilly would do the wheel between them; I was to go on watch at 20h00. This suited me fine because when we left Colombo for Aden on October 22, I didn't have to get up and turn to at 07h00, instead I stayed in my bunk until seven bells and turned to at 08h00. I'd never liked the peggy's job anyway, and all of a sudden there seemed to be a huge weight off my shoulders. Unfortunately, things went wrong on the first day out of Colombo. John Coyne the four to eight farmer had forgotten to pump up the water for the galley, added to which, he never filled the urn, made the tea, or put the breakfast plates into the galley on time. I couldn't help but think back a few weeks when I'd put him on the shake twenty minutes late, I could still hear his screams.

If it had been me who'd made so many errors, I'd have endured the wrath of the bosun and everybody who had suffered through my being half asleep; I'd also have been once more been threatened with dismissal from the Merchant Navy. However, and later in the day, the bosun told me in future I was to carry on with the peggying from 07h00 through to 12h00 and I was to get an hour's overtime. It wasn't really an hour's overtime I wanted, but I just had to do it; my overtime rate was one shilling and sixpence an hour which meant in financial terms, for every thirteen hours and twenty minutes worked, I'd receive £1.

By now I'd ceased the process of reconditioning tea leaves. My plan for some time had been to get back at those gentlemen in the Suez. As they were world-renowned for their underhandedness, I wanted to see if I could pull the wool over the eyes of one of them. My dearest wish with regard to the tea leaves, was to sell them to the person who'd sold Old Bill Orbell a bottle of cold tea on the outward passage.

During the forenoon on the second day out, I was given the job of scrubbing the runner mats which went the length of the mess room. Having done this job a few times before, I knew it wasn't much to do and I thought I'd take them aft and scrub them with a deck broom. At the time, Young George (he was only thirty-six) was off watch and sitting smoking on the bitts. After watching me making preparations for the scrubbing of the runners by laying them out on the deck, he told me I was wasting time and energy. He suggested I should make the carpet runner fast to the end of a heaving line, throw it over the side and leave it for half an hour or so. He also said after half an hour in the wake of the ship, it would be cleaner than I could ever have cleaned it with a scrubber. I'd seen this done before by the other greasers doing their cabin runners, and to make a bit of time I agreed. Making sure Fred Hodges didn't catch me, I went up forrard for one of the heaving lines neatly hung under the focs'le head. On my return aft I made the heaving line fast to the middle of the runner then threw it over the wall. I watched it bouncing up and down in the wake of the ship, lit a cigarette, and thanked George for his time saving suggestion. I went into the heads and bathrooms, and after cleaning them made tracks to make the smoko.

After smoko in which I'd had a sit down, a smoke and some coffee for a change, I returned aft to inspect the runner but was in for a horrible surprise. After pulling the heaving line inboard, I found the canvas hem on each end of the runner had worked loose and disappeared, the edges on each end of the runners had become frayed; and on top of all that, the runner was only clean in patches. When the bosun arrived on the scene and saw the result of my labour saving techniques he went berserk. I thought at first he was going to have a heart attack or a fit, but after he'd gathered himself, he told me for being so lazy I'd have to repair the damage in my own time. I was given some canvas, sail twine, and a palm and needle from Fred, who also told me off, then started the job after lunch. Although the job took the whole afternoon it was the first and last time I ever cleaned runners 'the engine room way'.

The eight to twelve works the same as the other two watches with three men in each. Two of the men will split the four hours by doing two hours each on the wheel, the other man who is known as the farmer will take the first wheel on the next watch. In this system of working, the three mens duties will rotate evenly. In my case things were a little different as I did the peggying in the forenoon watch, with Tug and Gilly splitting the forenoon wheels between them. In the night watch I would do one hour's lookout and two hours wheel, therefore I never did a night farmer.

The 'farmer' is the name given to the man in the watch who has no wheel to do. This name I've been told by Bill, stems from the times when a cattle boat was transporting cattle, and the owner of the livestock had to accompany his herd on the sea passage. As the owner or 'farmer' who was working his passage was unable or unqualified to steer the ship, he did the lookout instead. Therefore, the name of 'farmer,' the one who has no wheel to do during a watch, and the one who does the longest lookout, has come down through the ages.

Steering the ship is fine when learning or when there is no obligation or duty to do so, however after one has learned and is then duty bound it's not so exciting anymore; eventually it becomes downright boring. I remembered the time not so long ago when I was most eager to go on the wheel, by now the novelty had long since worn off, although it would no doubt be more exciting with the pilot on board.

After a man's been on the wheel for two hours and been watching the fingers on the wheel house clock move ever so slowly, he always welcomes his relief; but if his relief arrived just one minute late it can cause great resentment. I knew this because I'd heard some of them in the mess room complaining about each other behind their backs. I'd decided of all the faults I was told I possessed, I'd make sure that this one wasn't added to the list, therefore I always went on the wheel at five minutes before I was due. Some sailors judge their counterparts not on their working capabilities, or even their lifestyle in the mess, but on their compliance with time-keeping when relieving the wheel, and to some of them this is of paramount importance.

It seems to be an age old practice when after a voyage a ship approaches the UK, the vessel must arrive in pristine condition; this is apparently for the appeasement of the owners should they pay a visit to the vessel. Since I'd joined the ship, some things had changed with regards to the work I had to do and the work I used to do. This involved the polishing of the bright work and other similar jobs which were seldom done now. The reason was, as well as being a man short homeward bound, the bosun had found different work on deck for me. He wanted the *Willesden* 'Ship shape and Bristol fashion', so the well being of the accommodation had to suffer. Well, I'd much rather work on deck than be on my hands and knees for half the day.

One morning after smoko on the way to Aden, I was given the job of oiling the wooden decks on top of, and around the poop housing. On the outward passage I'd observed the chippy re-seaming some of the decks around the poop, finishing off by pouring boiling pitch into the seams. The oil I was to apply was an equal mixture of raw linseed oil and turps with a spoonful of red lead to enhance the colouring of the wooden decking. The oil was applied with a mop over all the wooden decks and the job didn't take long to complete. I'd been told the idea of oiling the wooden decks with such a mixture, is for the oil to seep into the wood which is three inches thick. This in turn will retard the drying out of the natural oil from the wood. It will also in the short term give the decks a pleasant smell as well as a fresh appearance. I felt as though I'd done something useful for a change when I'd finished, the after end of the ship smelled lovely and fresh with the linseed oiling. The good news for the day, was I didn't have to get up to do the pegging between 07h00 and 08h00 anymore, so now I could have an extra hour in my bunk

The second mate Mr. Brown and the two apprentices George Chell and Alister Kerr were checking all the stores in the lifeboats. They did one boat a day and had all the lifeboat rations and survival equipment carefully spread out on the boat deck. The water in the tanks was changed after those tanks had been given a thorough rinse out. I didn't think there were so many items in the boat, but everyone of them was checked against a list. George and Alister the apprentices looked very smart when they were in their uniforms, but when at sea there was no favoritism just because they were future officers. They had to earn their keep and get stuck in like everyone else. During the course of the voyage they quite often had to report to the bosun for deck work such as chipping and scraping. At times they'd been over the side on a stage as well as many other mundane jobs associated with the deck department. George once told me before he was to sit his second mate's ticket, he would have to pass his AB and Lifeboat Examination. I always got on well with George and I hoped after this trip we would be on the same ship again.

On arrival at Aden I couldn't help noticing the weather, although still hot, was quite a bit cooler than when we were outward bound. The sailors were as brown as berries with their constant working on deck whilst the stewards in comparison looked like bottles of milk. Those stewards would come out on deck from 13h00 to15h00 for some suntanning and each would bring a blanket, pillow, sunglasses, cigarettes and matches, and possibly a book to read. They would then stretch themselves out on the boat deck to catch the sun. Whenever I saw the stewards laying down getting suntanned, I always took great pleasure in quietly approaching one of them as he would be lying down with his eyes closed. I would then stand in such a way, blocking the sun from his body. The sleeping beauty would soon be aware the suns rays weren't reaching him, and thinking a passing cloud was the culprit, would open his eyes to see me standing there, I would then be told to 'go away' in a strange language that cannot be printed.

After working hours each day all hands would be occupying the showers and the compartment would often be full of naked bodies. It was rather comical to see those of the deck crowd who never wore shorts; their upper bodies would be tanned like Red Indians and their legs would be snow-white. None of the greasers ever wore shorts and by the appearance of their torsos only removed their shirts when showering. The greasers all walked around with a sweat rag around their neck as though it was part of an engine room uniform. Old Fred always wore a singlet and when he took it off he was so white underneath one would think he still had his singlet on. I asked Old Bill Orbell why he didn't come out on deck and get some sun, but he replied by saying he was past that phase of life and at fifty-five he was too old to get a girl. I told him of my suspicions he was nearer seventy, because I'd heard him speaking of a ship he'd been on in the year 1900. Bill just gave a little smile and winked.

Our stay in Aden was a short one, just long enough to take on bunkers and receive a flying visit from Abdullah the bumboat man, the ship then headed towards the Suez Canal. With each passing hour, somebody or other reminded me of Mustapha the boatman who would be awaiting my arrival in Port Teufiq.

One afternoon on our way up the Red Sea, the bosun told me to report to Fred who gave me a job burning out paint pots on the foredeck. In doing this I had to light a little fire inside each pot with a parafin soaked rag, then after all the hardened paint had become loose, scrape the rubbish from the pots and into a bucket. Later on, and by which time I'd filled up the bucket with the rubbish, I saw the bosun talking to Fred by the paint store. I began walking aft with the bucket to dump its contents over the wall, thinking at the same time I would be able to light up a cigarette and steal a few minutes, but it wasn't to be. The bosun who had been suspiciously watching my activities called me back and asked me where was I going, I told him I was going down aft to dump the trash over the wall. He asked me why didn't I stop wasting time and dump it over the side from the fore deck. My reply tinged with a little sarcasm, was on the previous voyage when I'd emptied a bucket of dirty water over the wall from amidships, I'd been told by him to always dump anything overboard from aft. To add to the sarcasm and by reiterating his own words, I told him about a deck boy I'd heard about who'd thrown an old runner wire over the wall which had caught in the prop. The bosun wasn't very impressed with my temerity and remarked on my insolence. He then told me in a highly agitated voice on the ship's arrival in the UK, he would be personally presenting me with a free railway voucher, which implied once again I was to be sacked. The bosun then grabbed the bucket of paint scrapings and emptied them off the fore deck over the wall, before ordering me back to work.

At this time all the deck crowd were working overtime painting the ship; Bill Houston had previously shown me how to rig myself in a bosun's chair, and because of this I was to assist in painting the funnel. First I was sent inside the funnel with John Dick, then after climbing up the inside ladder we went through a trap door at the top. It was really hot up there and with all the smoke and carbon blowing around I thought I wouldn't like to stay up too long. We pulled the funnel blocks up with the gantlines already rove through, then positioned the funnel blocks on the rim of the funnel casing; we were both filthy being covered in carbon.

After going below again the next thing was for me to sit in the chair, then pull myself up and make myself fast. When I got to the top I felt a bit nervous in case I might put the hitch on wrong, but John Coyne who was tending, held on to the lower end until I was satisfied I had it right. To me the funnel didn't look very high when standing on the quay, but when sitting in a chair on top it looks an awful long way down; in fact the funnel itself was twenty-eight feet tall. I had two buckets of water I'd pulled up, and made them fast on each side of the chair; one was soda for washing all the carbon off, the other one was fresh for rinsing. I was doing the center fleet, Paddy Dolan, Mick Bayes, and Bill Houston were doing the fleets on after end of me, John Cunningham and John Dick the forrard side, Gilly was doing the ladder fleet, John Coyne was tending and Tug Wilson was on the wheel. After we'd gone down a few feet the water in my bucket was so filthy it had to be changed. The soojy job was finished before lunch time.

At 13h00 the job of painting the funnel began. I was left out for this part of the operation because the bosun implied I always spilled more paint than I put on the part to be painted, saying an extra man would be required to go over my holidays and clean up after me. This statement by the bosun was an exaggeration because I'd never done much painting on the ship before. The truth of the matter was, he'd used me for the worst part of the job in setting the funnel blocks. When the funnel was completed later in the afternoon, instead of being a drab colour, it was a glistening black and looked very smart.

Fred was on the go all the time in the paint locker and didn't knock off till 20h00 each day, he told me he was always preparing the materials for the next job. Next day Fred gave me the job of sweeping the fore deck, this was in preparation for it being painted with boot topping red. As the bit of wind was blowing from ahead, I started forrard and began working my way aft. Someway down the deck the wind changed direction and came from aft. I then swept from aft to forrard but the blustery turbulent wind changed again and again, it took me an hour to do a job that should have been done in twenty minutes. 'Shipshape and Bristol fashion' was quick to remind me I'd taken far too long to do the job and wouldn't accept any explanation I gave him.

During the past couple of months I'd made myself busy collecting all the dried out tea leaves and putting them in a neatly made sack with a bit of genuine tea on top. Now the ship was approaching the Suez Canal I'd carefully sewn the little sack up to make it look 'manufactured' and kept it in my bottom drawer.

The Suez Boatmen

We arrived at Port Teufiq at daybreak, and to my great surprise there was Mustapha in his boat with a new companion. When he saw me he waved an admonishing finger as if to say I had greatly offended him. All the ships which traverse the Suez Canal carry four boats, and despite the prophesies as to my death, I'd always thought it highly unlikely we would get the same boatmen; but there he was, a very irate Mustapha. I later learned the agent acting on behalf of the P&O Line to whom the *Willesden* was chartered, used the same boatmen for all the P&O ships. At Port Teufiq we were all sitting on number four hatch having smoko. The greasers were all talking about a ship called the *Georgic* which had been bombed there and I think it was Old Albert who said he was on it at the time. Fred Hodges had his camera out and was taking photographs of a ship called the *World Glory* which was 56,000 tons and supposed to be the biggest tanker in the world.

The four boats were hoisted on board, and as soon as Mustapha had the chance and much to the crowd's amusement he approached me. He told me because I hadn't let his boat go on the outward passage, the vessel had become damaged in the bouncing up and down of the ship's wake. He continued by saying he'd been held responsible and had to pay for the repairs to much of the planking. I was amused but tried not to show it, and asked him to show me the repairs on the boat (which I knew was owned by the Suez Canal Company). He told me he couldn't, this was a different boat and the damaged one was still under repair.

In trying to gain some sympathy, he told me his house had been burgled and the robbers had taken what little he owned. He pleaded with me asking if could I help him out financially, or even give him something he could sell. I gave him some food which had been left over from the breakfast and this action was greeted with a chorus of skits from the crowd; they also said I should give him a £1 compensation for his previous discomfort, and another £1 for the repairs to his boat. By now the ship was on the move through the canal, there was a BTC tanker and an Anglo Saxon tanker ahead, then a German cargo ship and an 'A' class Blue Funnel boat astern of us, these were the only ships I could see.

I'd been hoping we'd make a night passage through the canal then I could possibly go on the wheel. In the forenoon watch when I was peggy, I wasn't even allowed to give a smoko to Tug Wilson. So after taking him a cup of coffee, I hung around the wheelhouse to take notice of all the goings on. There were two pilots, Captain Grist, the third mate, George Chell, as well as Tug in the wheelhouse. The ship was making the maximum six knots speed allowed, otherwise and as George had told me, if the ship went any faster it would wash away the banks of the canal, he then whispered to me I should leave the bridge before the captain saw me.

On the outward passage we'd had a searchlight hung off over the stem, this time there was to be no searchlight, the canal passage had been planned to take place during the hours of daylight. The ship arrived at the Bitter Lakes just before lunch time then anchored. We were to remain there until the south bound convoy passed us that night. It was a real pleasure to finish the peggy's job at 12h00, a little luxury I'd never known before, and with all that water to swim in. I'd be off until 20h00 and after lunch time I went with many of the crew for a swim; I didn't want to work overtime like the others and kept well away from the ship. I stayed in the water for most of the afternoon, and had many a dive from the wing of the bridge. When I climbed back aboard I received a scowl from the bosun for not offering my services, he told me for being so lazy I wouldn't be considered for any more overtime. Later on I did a swop with Mustapha, and to recompense him for his previous hardship I let him have a good deal. He gave me two brass statues, one of Neffertiti, and the other of Tutenkamen, this was in exchange for my 25/- utility suit which had by now become far too small for me. When the crowd in the messroom heard of the transaction, I was given a chorus of unpleasantries for selling a suit they said was worth a £1 for a pair of rubbish statues valued at 1/- each, and all because I was afraid of getting my throat slit by Mustapha.

Mustapha's companion had some Port Said postcards for sale and I'd already seen him offering them to one of the greasers before asking me did

I want to buy them. He was another of those whose father had been born in Liverpool and like all the rest couldn't remember from which district. After making inquiries, he said he wanted £5 for the set of ten, however because I was from Liverpool he'd consider letting them go a bit cheaper at £3. I asked him for a closer examination, but he would only let me look at a couple of them from a distance. Naturally I said that the photographs were overpriced and they could be obtained much cheaper elsewhere, moreover, I had no money.

Mustapha's friend and boat mate who's name I couldn't pronounce, could see I was interested and asked if I couldn't get something from the mess to pay for them. He suggested knives, forks, spoons crockery, sheets, towels or anything else which could be used in lieu of the £3. I pretended to think hard, then said I could possibly steal a seven pound bag of tea from the second steward. It was my turn to see a glimmer of interest in my adversary's eye, and he agreed to have a look at the tea. A little later a rendezvous was made where an examination of the tea could take place which may then lead to a transaction. The cloak-and-dagger deal was to take place during the hours of darkness by his boat – mainly to avoid my being caught with the 'stolen' tea.

By late afternoon, the crowd from 'Ull on't River 'Umber knew of the forthcoming deal to be struck on the afterdeck. They were all aware for a couple of months I'd been planning this little episode and even marvelled at the quality appearance of the 'reconditioned' tea leaves. To give an added incentive to any prospective buyer, I'd even sprinkled a few ounces of real tea on top of the rubbish for added aroma. At the time I'd only told them about the postcards to create some amusement, however I was soon to regret opening my big mouth to anyone.

At about 20h00 we were still at anchor in the Bitter Lakes, and after watching the south bound convoy pass in procession with their navigation lights on, I met the boatman by number five hatch. He looked at the tea bag and immediately declared I was trying to cheat him. He said I'd told him it was a seven-kilo bag of tea, and not the seven-pound bag I had in my hand. He went on to say unless I could produce a similar bag of tea as well, or come up with something else, the deal was off.

I'd been expecting some bartering of this kind and after showing my disappointment turned to go away. I declared it was impossible for me to get any more tea and I'd have to return this bag before it was missed. However, before I'd gone a few steps he relented saying he would at least examine the tea, then maybe I could get something else to swing the deal. The stitching of the tea bag was then partly removed and the owner of the photographs had a little sniff and a feel of the contents before he shook his head saying what I had was crew tea and he would be losing out on the deal.

The haggling went on during which he told me his photos were worth £5, and it was only because I was from Liverpool, the same place as his father, he'd already reduced the price and was doing me a great favour. He continued by saying the tea was probably only worth about 10/-; ship's tea, and especially for the sailors' mess was always of poor quality (the only correct statement he made). The transaction was not completed.

Next morning at 05h00 the ship weighed anchor and we were on the move again. It was just before we arrived at Port Said when the boatman cracked. He approached me by knocking on the mess room porthole saying he'd given a lot of thought to the matter and would agree to the deal but on one condition – which was on the following voyage I was to give him a further 10/-. I had a strong feeling within me, even if the boatman knew I was due for the sack, he'd still have taken the tea. The deal was finally struck and shortly before he was lowered over the side in his boat, the hand-over was completed. As soon as I got the chance I went into the pantry to examine the photographs, just as I suspected there were only eight in the pack. Then just as I was about to show them to the cabin boys who'd arrived at great speed, a hand came from behind snatching them from me. It was Old Albert! He was livid, and threatened to take me up to the captain as soon as he came off the bridge.

At Port Said the ship went to the buoys, number three and four hatches were stripped to load a few tons of cargo for Beiruit, which comprised of bales of cotton goods which went into the 'tween decks. A couple of hours later the ship was on the move again heading for the unscheduled Lebanese port.

As we passed De Lessops statue at the Port Said breakwater, I was just going into the after accommodation when Old Albert called me over. In his hand he held the photos he'd taken from me, and I thought he was now going to march me up to the captain's cabin. Instead he ripped them up in front of me and threw the bits over the wall; he told me I should be ashamed of myself. I told Old Albert I didn't want the photos anyway, the objective had only been to see if I could pull the wool over the eyes of the notorious boatmen, and it had worked. Some time later and after conferring with the cabin boys, I wondered if the old swine had examined the photos in detail before he'd ripped them up. Later still, I wondered if they were the same photos, or were they just bits of paper he'd ripped up keeping the real photos for him-

Above: The *Malakand* of T&J Brocklebanks, lay astern of us in London's Victoria Dock.

Below: The previous *Malakand*.
One of the biggest disasters in the Port of Liverpool during the Second World War was the explosion of the *Malakand* in May 1941.

SS *Novelist*. She was at anchor with us at Aden.

Above: The *Baron Inverclyde*. She was hungry.

Below: The *Sekondi,* also hungry but at least we had water to drink.

Above: SS *Twickenham*. Captain Grist. the bosun and Fred Hodges previously served on this ship.

Below: SS *Indian City*. This was the ship on which the second cook Peter Kingham last served.

Above: *SS Velutina*. Was she the first supertanker?

Below: *Roonagh Head*
She was in Montreal with us.

Above: Taken in 1999. Fred Hodges (on the left) receiving, posthumously on behalf of the bosun, the painting the author had promised him forty-six years previously.

Above: The ill fated *Pamir* lay across the River Elbe from us in 1953

Below: *Passat*. Also on the River Elbe in 1953. She is now a museum ship in Sweden

Name of

PARTICULARS

Reference No.	Income Tax Code.	SIGNATURES OF CREW AND NUMBERS OF DISCHARGE BOOKS. 1.	Age. 2.	* Nationality (if British, state birthplace—see footnote). 3.	ADDRESSES OF MASTER AND CREW. NAME AND RELATIONSHIP OF NEXT OF KIN OR NAME OF FRIEND AND HOME ADDRESS. 4.	Name of last Ship, with Official No. or Port of Registry and year of discharge if more than a year previous. 5.	Date and Place of Signing this Agreement. Date. 6.	Place. 7.
41	51732 S.	S. Williams R415824	29	London	(1) Guardian Mrs D. Stait (2) 215 [illegible] Southend	Dryden	23/11/53	Tilbury
42	U S.	Curren E1682	23	Dublin	(1) W. Margaret (2) 38 Glendown Rd. [illegible]	Leckenham	"	do
43	5064 S.	A. Gibbs R502228	21	Grays	(1) F. Charles (2) 21 Factory Rd. Grays	Busen Rollo	"	"
44	65 M	[illegible] R83413	63	[illegible]	(1) Wife: Elizabeth (2) 50 St. Chads Rd Tilbury	Ninella	24/11/53	Tilbury
45	S	Walker 426819	67	[illegible]	Brother [illegible] Edinburgh South west Scotland	[illegible]	"	do
46	65 S	[illegible] R399884	[illegible]	[illegible]	Mother Mrs A. [illegible] 106 [illegible]	Regent Hawk	"	"
47	52 M.	[illegible] R190139	31	Dunbar	Mr. [illegible] 24 Countess Rd Dunbar	Greenwich	7/12/53	Hull
48	S	J. R. Kane R598496	28	West Hartlepool	(1) M. Jessie (2) 78 [illegible] Rd. M'bro.	Brackley Moor	8/12/53	Hull.
49	S	[illegible] R583551	22	Kylin Colenham	(1) F. Donald (2) 89 Westbourne Ave, [illegible]	LA Grieves	do	do
50	S	P W Wesson R364605	22	London	(1) M. Mary (2) 68 [illegible] House, London	[illegible]	8/12/53	Hull
51					(1) (2)			
52					(1) (2)			
53					(1) (2)			
54					(1) (2)			
55					(1) (2)			
56					(1) (2)			
57					(1) (2)			
58					(1) (2)			
59					(1) (2)			
60					(1) (2)			

* If a British subject, state town or country of birth, and if born in a foreign

† The capacities of Engineers not employed on the Propelling Engines and Boilers should be described here and in the Certificate of Discharge as Engine Drivers, Donkeymen, should be described as

‡ If the advance of wages is not conditional on going to sea

§ If any member of the Crew enters Her Majesty's Service, the Name of the Queen's Ship into which he enters is to be stated under the head of "Cause of Leaving

** **NATIONAL INSURANCE.—The Master and all members of the crew are insurable under the National Insurance Schemes. Masters should ensure that issued by the Ministry of National Insurance.**

On the above articles the name of R. Walker is recorded. He gave his age as sixty-seven. The author later discovered he was probably eighty-seven.

self. Either way I knew it was an offence I'd committed, and Captain Grist wouldn't have been very pleased. Some of the sailors said Old Albert had no right doing what he'd done, but it served me right anyway; they said by now the poor boatman would have sold the tea, and would later receive a good thrashing from its buyer.

The ship arrived at Beiruit early on Saturday and the two hatches were stripped for the discharge of the Port Said cargo. It wasn't as though there was a lot of cargo, but some of the crowd were worried we might miss a Sunday at sea if no dockers worked the weekend.

The bosun told me as the ship was now in port, I was to resume the peggy's duties. Acting on the advice of Tug and Gilly, I asked the bosun for clarification on the payment of overtime for working the Saturday afternoon. He answered saying I wasn't entitled to it because I was still the peggy; he further told me I was lucky he'd let me go in the eight to twelve watch. I told him it wasn't in the union rules about being a peggy and in a watch at the same time. The bosun absolutely blew. He said I was a typical scouse mess deck lawyer and asked to whom I'd been talking to come up with such a statement. The final result of my inquiry, was the watch on deck had to do the peggying at teatime and I didn't get any more overtime for the trip. This didn't bother me at all as it meant I had more time for drawing.

We left Beiruit on the Sunday morning and we got our full Sunday at sea. The weather was a bit cold and next day when Paddy Dolan came off the wheel he found his mongoose dead. Poor Paddy was upset, and in a shoe box weighted down with a shackle, Sam was buried at sea.

Bill Houston often showed me things and today I learned something else. He had an old gaberdine raincoat which he painted all over the outside with boiled linseed oil, then hung it under the focs'le head. Next day it was dry and Bill said it was quite waterproof and OK for working in during the rain or for doing the lookout.

I only had one presentable pair of dungaree trousers which I wore when going on the wheel. As well as them, I had the shorts I'd been measured up for in Calcutta, and the shorts I'd been wearing all the trip. As the weather had now changed, I sewed the legs back on the dungaree shorts and they looked quite comical. The upper part which had been my working shorts had faded with the dhobying they'd received and were covered in paint, while the half-mast legs which were sewn back on were quite new. When the bosun saw me with my reconditioned dungarees he failed to see the comical side and made unfavourable comments about my painting abilities. He said there was more paint on my dungaree shorts than there was on the ship's side.

I had only one pair of socks which hadn't been worn since we'd left London, and I dug them out remembering they needed darning on the heels, however as soon as I started on them in the recreation room, the skits began. I was accused of having the channels. Just for a laugh I answered my tormentors by saying I didn't have the channels, only wanting to get off this old rust bucket and it was the worst ship I'd ever been on (ie the only ship). Just then the doorway of the recreation room was filled with the shape of the bosun. He'd overheard my speech and his face was a mask of anger, he demanded to know where the rust bucket was. Knowing he took some pride in his job and the appearance of the ship, I said I was only joking. He didn't see it my way and once again I was informed on the ship's arrival at the first UK port, I was to be discharged.

The skies were blue all the way across the Med, and the temperature in the daytime was quite nice although at night it became a bit cold. Nevertheless, I told myself, I'd rather have this weather than the heat of the Red Sea in August. On November 14 Captain Grist sent for Bill Houston and told him because of his exemplary conduct during the voyage, he was cancelling the loggings he'd received for missing the ship at Newcastle Quay. Bill was of course delighted, and later told us at first when the captain called him, he'd feared some bad news from home. There was no mention of Big Ron, Jim Dawson or John Levitt being granted a reprieve from their loggings.

Passing through the Straight of Gibraltar and out into the Atlantic, the sky remained blue and even most of the way through the Bay of Biscay, but when the ship reached Ushant the sky was grey and the weather cold. By now everyone on deck was wearing long trousers, jerseys, and coats, the bleak grey skies and the cold were the sign which said 'welcome back to the UK'.

The ship was in a very clean condition and it reminded me of the very first day I'd stepped aboard six months previously. A few ships were seen going up and down the English Channel and I noted the further up the channel we went, the greater the volume of shipping. The wind was quite cold coming from the north-east and at one time while I was soojying the winches on the fore deck, the wind whipped the spray right up over the port shoulder and I was soaked through. I was dying to tell the bosun about the three winch beds that hadn't been cleaned – I couldn't wait for pay-off day.

Tilbury Dock

The ship was now preparing for London, we pulled the ropes up and coiled them on the focs'le head, then did the after ropes which were in the lazarette. The pilot came aboard at Beachy Head and in the River Thames the mud pilot took over. On a cold grey misty day, early on November 23 the ship tied up at Tilbury Dock. The derricks had already been topped in the river, the hatches were stripped once the ship was alongside, and the dockers were soon discharging general cargo from the 'tween decks. There is always some excitement on arrival at a port by some of the crowd with regards to mail. It didn't bother me one bit as I hadn't written or had a letter from anyone during the whole trip; therefore I wasn't expecting any mail, however today I received a letter from the Ministry of Pensions and National Insurance confirming my National Insurance number. The chippy wasn't so lucky though, he hadn't had a letter during the whole trip; he had no known family, or so he said! The bosun was often quite amusing, he was always asking him who he was going to leave all his money to when he pegged out. The only time the chippy had ever been ashore was to connect up the water pipes from shore to ship or to record the draught marks. I knew quite well the bosun was only joking when he cast such caustic aspersions on the chippy being extra careful with his money. Although at the same time I thought he was obviously quite rich, it was his own want. I thought back to all the money I'd wasted on chocolate and fruit juice during the voyage and wished in a way I'd been a bit more careful like Achmid.

At about 09h45, I was walking up the after deck to make the smoko when on the quayside I espied none other than the bosun. He was dressed to the nines and sheltering from the rain in an alcove with a suitcase by his side.

At first I didn't recognise him, as he stood there waiting for someone or something. I'd only ever seen him dressed in dungarees, blue denim shirt and his little cap; but now he looked quite dapper in his grey suit and polished shoes. I didn't know what was happening but was soon to discover the bosun and Fred Hodges were paying off in view of their making a come-back on the following voyage. The bosun was waiting for Fred to finish paying off, and I was absolutely stunned at the pair's unheralded departure. Later on when I went to my cabin I found all Fred's gear had gone (stowed away in the bosun's cabin) and his bedding returned to the second steward. Bill Houston was promoted to bosun.

Also paying off but under different and rather harrowing circumstances were Big Ron and Jim Dawson, this was no doubt due to the disturbance in Colombo where they'd both been logged. I never found out if they were charged in court, I just hope they weren't, but according to the galley wireless they both received a DR in their books. The chief steward Mr. Perkins also paid off and unfortunately I never had the chance to say goodbye to him either.

Later in the morning our new bosun introduced me to my new cabin mate. I'd had so many shocks and surprises during the day with people coming and going, however this was the best of all. My new cabin mate was an old Scotsman named either Bob or Stan Walker. He greeted me with such cordiality, it was like someone meeting a friend he hadn't seen for years. In my opinion Stan must have been at least seventy-five years old, however except for a bit of a hobble he was quite lively as he made his way around. It was really nice to meet Stan, who Bill the new bosun immediately 'promoted' to peggy. All the dockers knew Stan and of his many previous escapades. It wasn't long before Stan was telling me of his past, how he'd started his sea career aged twelve on the fishing boats before going deep sea on the big square riggers. He either didn't know or else he wouldn't tell me how old he was, but said the authorities had him down for sixty-seven; a figure he appeared quite happy to accept.

Also signed on was Stan Williams who was to replace Bill Houston who had replaced Sam Barter the bosun. So now with the two new signings we had an 'Old Stan' and a 'Young Stan'. They were only here for the run around the land and would be paying off at Middlesborough with the rest of us, but what a lively pair they turned out to be.

Old Stan must have received an advance note when signing on, because after making his acquaintances and throwing his gear in the cabin, he awarded himself the afternoon off.

At 13h00 Bill Houston asked me if I'd seen him, but I could only reply I hadn't. In the mess room I asked the dockers, who all seemed to know him, if they'd seen him, they were highly amused. They said once Old Stan had money in his pocket he'd be in the nearest pub. They also told me Old Stan, or Uncle Bob as he was also known around the London docks, had served in sail for many years and had even sailed in the *Cutty Sark*, on her last voyage under the red ensign. Later on in the mess room the dockers also told us Old Stan hadn't been deep sea for many a year, he was far past his best, and just took stand-bys, around the land, gangway watchman, or run jobs. Once again I was the peggy for the rest of the day, however there seemed to be an air of relaxation now that His Lordship Mr. Barter had gone on leave.

In the evening I went to the cinema with Ron Stafford. Outside in the foyer there was a weighing machine and I was curious to know just how much weight I'd put on since I'd joined the ship. I had an overcoat on (my lookout coat) and what were once my parade boots, but even so, I topped the scales at ten stone four. I reckoned the clothes I wore weighed ten pounds, which meant, I'd put on twenty-two pounds of weight in six months; and I still wasn't fat! After the film show where the police caught all the robbers and locked them up, we dashed along to the next cinema. There we saw a film in which John Wayne was a submarine commander, he destroyed the Japanese fleet and won the Pacific War. Ron and I went back to the ship after the 'flix' and I turned in thinking the night was over. But it wasn't . . . not by a long shot. Sometime after midnight I was woken up by the shore gangway watchman who asked me if I knew an old man named Stan Walker, because if I did, he was flaked out drunk at the top of the companionway. Old Stan was quite a heavy man and weighed about twelve stone; eventually he was manhandled below, but it took George Chafer, the watchman and myself to do it. Once in the cabin Uncle Stan came to and started singing sea shanties, and try as we might, we just couldn't shut him up. Unfortunately he'd woken the whole of the crowd singing in his Scotch gravel voice before flaking out again. We made his bunk up and after a bit of a struggle took his boots off. I was sadly shocked when I discovered the poor old man wore steel calipers on both his legs.

Next morning I tried to wake Old Stan. He was still and cold so I covered his face and went up on deck to tell somebody. There was a bit of a pandemonium as everyone crowded into the cabin to see the corpse for themselves, but on our arrival there was Old Stan sitting on the edge of his bunk.

I got the height of abuse from the crowd for proclaiming Old Stan had pegged out. The old man in question didn't seem a bit bothered and had a good laugh about it. He said he wasn't going so easy, and informed me in his strong Scottish accent he was ready to face the world for another day. I later told the bosun what had happened in the small hours, about the sea shanties we'd been entertained to, and about Old Stan's legs having iron calipers on them. As the bosun, poor Bill who was already a man short on deck now had Old Stan to contend with, and who, despite his eager efforts wasn't capable of much. As Curly Megginson had never been replaced this made us two men short on deck, but Bill Houston being the type of man he was, didn't report him. He knew Old Stan was on his last legs as a sailor, and he'd be paid off before we sailed and may not ever get another ship. In the light of those circumstances, and because the ship would hardly be at sea for long periods, I suppose Bill thought Old Stan could be carried. Therefore, I did the peggy's job again completing only the bare essentials, before turning to on deck.

We hadn't seen rain for months, but since sighting the first UK landfall at Beachy Head, it had hardly stopped and when there wasn't rain or drizzle there was fog. The best way to describe the British weather after all the sun we'd had, was gloomy, dreary and depressing. Two days after our arrival in London we sailed again for Antwerp, we had the pilot on board all the way, and this I was told was due to the ship having no radar. The run to Antwerp was expected to take less than twenty-four hours, and for this reason the derricks were just lowered into their crutches with the guys remaining set. By now Old Stan had made a full recovery from his advance note party, and never could a more willing man be seen. He had no intentions of being a passenger and did his best even if it was only to wash the plates, keep the mess room and pantry tidy and give everyone a good laugh. He had tried to scrub the deck in the messroom, but I told him a sixteen year old was much more suited to the job. As I looked at Stan with his weather-beaten face, hands like shovels and a pair of shoulders like a barn door, I would have loved to read his life story. Bosun Bill was always talking to him about old sailing ships – and that's where the two had a lot in common.

The Continent

The weather in Antwerp was just like London, grey and dreary with the same rain pattern. There wasn't much cargo to be discharged at the port, and although we were only in for one night, what a night it turned out to be. I received a sub from our new chief steward and went ashore with the two cabin boys. I wore my new, expensive shoes which I'd bought in London for 30/- however they were hurting my heels. After walking around a bit exploring the city, we were invited into a club by one of the locals. He said he'd like to extend the warm feelings of his country, and would like to buy us all a drink. We went downstairs into the night-club where I had a glass of beer. Our host sat with us and shortly afterwards we were joined at the table by two of his friends. The lights were low and I saw some women were dancing together, at first I thought nothing of this but when I saw them kissing each other I thought they were lesbians which I'd heard of. Then I saw two men dancing, and became even more suspicious, and when they began kissing each other my suspicions were confirmed. We were soon to discover, all the 'women' were in fact men dressed up in girls' clothes and wearing lipstick – it was a 'men only' club we were in. We didn't stay long and had a good laugh about it on the way back but by the time we arrived at the ship I was hobbling, my heels were skinned to the bone with my new shoes.

The ship left Antwerp on the evening of November 28, arriving at Hamburg on the 30th. We were tied up at what must have been a smelting factory and there were huge piles of scrap iron all along the quayside. Right by our gangway, there was a thirty-foot mound of rusty unused gunnery shells which the Wehrmacht never had the chance to fire. This was the first time I'd ever seen real 'rounds' of ammunition. Old Stan did quite well for a man who was crippled, he was always trying to come out on deck to help but the bosun wouldn't let him, telling him instead what a good job he was doing in the messroom.

Once again I got a sub for which I received eleven marks and seventy pfennigs to the pound. We tied up in the River Elbe where I had a good look around the docks and where the visible signs of the Second World War were still evident; the war had been over for eight years by now, and there was a lot of re-building going on all around. At teatime I saw the bosun talking to the shore gangway man to whom I was later introduced. His name was Hans, was well-built and aged about fifty-five; I noticed when speaking he stood very erect and was neatly dressed, his trousers were well pressed and he wore a naval greatcoat. Hans had the air of a man of authority and spoke perfect English; so good in fact, if I hadn't been told, I'd have thought he was an Englishman.

As soon as Hans had gone up the deck, bosun Bill told me Hans had previously been a ship's captain, but because of the war, and now with the lack of work in Germany, he'd been reduced to being a ship's watchman. The bosun asked me to go and see if I could get him a meal from the galley, which I did. Hans was most grateful for the meal and displayed perfect manners. Later on Bosun Bill was engaged in talking to Hans about ships while I got ready to go ashore with the cabin boys.

On departing the ship at about 19h30, we went to the notorious red-light district of Herbert Strasse; this street was in the Cabbage Patch area of Hamburg. On arrival at our destination, we found the street was off limits to all British servicemen and was boarded off with corrugated sheet metal at both ends. At the top of the street there were three on-duty soldiers who stood denying entry to anyone who looked like a soldier. When we attempted to go through the narrow opening leading into the street, one of the soldiers who thought we were national servicemen forbade our entry. We told him we were in the Merchant Navy, not in the army and demanded access; he wouldn't let us through and called his sergeant over. On production of our seamen's identity cards, the sergeant took us aside. His accent told me he was from the same city as myself and after agreeing to let us through he gave us a warning, telling us of the dangers which lurked behind the corrugated iron partition. He said if we partook in a romp with any of the girls, then as sure as he was talking to us, we'd be seeing the doctor within a couple of weeks. Then he told us this was the reason the street was out of bounds to the British military. Before we went through the opening he wagged his finger at us, "Have a good look, but don't touch."

I found Herbert Strasse to be about forty yards long, consisting of a row of gardenless terrace type houses on each side with the front window of each house resembling a shop. A number of scantily clad women were in the windows of these houses, some having two temptresses per window and others three or four. Most of them were dressed in just panties and bra, a suspender belt, or something else to make them alluring to the passers-by. All the spectators were men and there were hundreds of them. Walking down one side of the street, I saw the girls were doing their best to entice the 'window shoppers' in for a frolic. The one attracting the most attention was a blonde girl with hair down to her waist. She was dressed in a pair of shiny high heeled boots, black stockings, with panties, bra and a studded belt to match. But what made her the draw of the street, was she also had a black whip, in case any masochists in the crowd wanted to pay for a bit of pain. We watched in awe at this window until a customer who's eye she caught went through the door. We hung around waiting to see how long he was going to spend with her and within fifteen minutes the client had emerged from her front door. The 'lady in black' then sat back on her perch brandishing the whip.

Each time I was asked to come in by one of the business ladies, I always asked them in sign language how much. The fee for their services was ten marks for the older or less attractive ones, or twenty for the younger or better lookers. There must have been a lot of masochists in the street because I saw the lady with the whip entertain three clients within the hour.

Well it was a night to remember if ever there was one. We all obeyed the sergeant, by looking but not touching so none of us would be making an appointment with the doctor.

I was scrubbing the bathrooms out the next morning at 09h00 when one of the sailors who'd belatedly arrived on board came in for a shower. I couldn't but help notice his back as he stripped off and was rather shocked at the state of it. He was ripped to ribbons, looking as though he'd been dragged backwards over a barbed wire fence. Well if that was a shock looking at his back, worse was to come when he told me of his previous night adventures. He said a nympho woman he'd stayed with had caused the lacerations, and tonight he was seeing her again.

In the afternoon Old Stan did the disappearing act and although the bosun knew he'd gone for a drink he wasn't missed. Young Stan got logged though, he never came aboard at all and was hit for two days' pay

After teatime, Hans the gangway watchman came aboard and I had a nice meal awaiting him. He was pleased with the meal although when I tried to give him a couple of packs of cigarettes he wouldn't take them. There was an air of pride about the man. Later on the bosun, Hans and myself stood out on the deck. Hans pointed across the river to two sailing ships, one was the *Pamir*, the other *Passat*. He said both ships were undergoing refits and would soon be sailing on commercial voyages. I never found out the history of Hans, but it would appear to me from the way he stood so erect and his general appearance he'd been in the Kreigsmarine.

We left Hamburg on December 3 after having discharged half of the iron ore cargo, the ship then proceeded to Hull. There was no more painting to be done owing to the dismal damp weather, and so it was soojying all the way across the North Sea. We were at sea for three days during which time and because he'd been adrift so much, everyone was having a laugh at Old Stan congratulating him for staying aboard each day we were at sea. The ship arrived at Hull on December 6, Mr. Kirby the mate went on leave and was replaced by Mr. Robertson, John Levitt had the logging he'd received in Colombo cancelled. Later, someone told me Big Ron the ex-cook and the assistant steward Jim Dawson had come aboard, unfortunately I never saw them. Many of the crowd originated from Hull and they mostly disappeared early on, so in the evening I had to go ashore alone. Only a small amount of cargo was to be discharged at Hull, consisting of bundles of coir or jute.

The Last Leg

Staying at Hull for two days, we left on December 9 on what was to be the last and shortest leg of our voyage, we tied up at Middlesboro the same evening, and after five months and two days the voyage was over. It was 18h00 by the time we'd finished tying up and the bosun told me I was no longer responsible for peggying, in fact I didn't have to do anything anymore, my wages had stopped when we'd finished tying up. We then had what someone called the last supper at 18h30 – a nice meal of steak, egg and chips. I took great pleasure in doing the washing-up before scrubbing the mess out for the last time.

In the evening there was a party in the recreation room, everyone was there with not a seat to be had; Old Stan was in fine form singing sea shanties and had a real go at the beer. There were lots of crates of beer and I was kept busy running back and forth to the chief steward for more cases which cost 18/- each. There were sing-songs all night and everyone reminisced about the now completed voyage. I was asked to do a one-man band demonstration, but I was much wiser now than I had been six months ago and sober too. It seemed none of the deck crowd were coming back for another voyage, and after some of the recent escapades in Hamburg I was not the only one to get the sack. During the party I was asked about my drawings and the diaries I'd been keeping. I stated the drawings I'd done had been given a passage in the North Sea, but I was keeping the diary so one day I could write a story about the voyage. I had a good laugh when the sailor who'd received the 'souvenir' from Newcastle, implored me not to mention his name in the book. In turn I told him it wouldn't be getting printed until the end of the century, and he'd have to wait nearly fifty years, by which time he'd be a little old man with a white beard using a walking stick, and probably wouldn't care anyway. Later on everybody was drunk and shaking hands with each other saying their good-byes and hoping they'd meet up again. I really thought the crowd had been good to me during the voyage and just hoped all crowds were the same.

I rose early the next morning and cleared the recreation room of all the empty bottles and ash trays, then scrubbed the place out for the last time. We were off wages and weren't really entitled to any breakfast, but we all had our usual meal, I then washed up also for the last time.

At 10h00 we assembled outside the saloon to be paid off; the men who had been my shipmates for the past five months looked quite different now. Gone were the dungarees, the singlets and sweat rags of the engine room crowd; gone also were the seaboots, oilskins and the sheathed knives which were every sailor's attire. They were now dressed in suits and I had to look at them twice to ascertain who each one was. The chippy wore a trilby, as did Old Albert who also had a gold watch and chain in his waistcoat pocket. At the paying off table I received £14 - 5s - 9d, my reward for a five months and two day voyage. There was no income tax deducted from my pay for the obvious reason I didn't earn enough. I also had sixteen days' leave to take as well as the free railway warrant which the bosun had so faithfully promised me.

Everybody was busy running around so I said my good-byes to those I could, knowing they would all be all heading for the nearest pub, I quietly slipped ashore. As I stepped onto the gangway I had the same funny feeling I'd felt when first joining the ship in South Shields; this time it was a kind of a sad empty feeling as though I was being separated with nowhere to go. I'd heard lots of tales in the messroom though, tales of better ships and different runs to go on; at the same time I told myself if all places were as bad as India I wouldn't go to sea any more.

With my suitcase containing all my worldly possessions and my £14 -5s - 9d I made my way across an iron swing bridge which I'd been told led to the railway station. There I stopped to have one last look at the ship which had been my home for the past seven months, wondering if I'd ever see her again.

I'd been at the railway station for ten minutes when Stan Williams came running up quite breathless. "Peggy," he said. "We've been looking everywhere..... we passed the hat around and collected seven pounds, ten shillings for you." I was absolutely dumbstruck and asked him what was it for. He told me the peggy always received something from the crowd, for unpaid overtime and the next trip I'd be on it would be my turn to chip in for the peggy.

So ended my second trip to sea. It was really an awakening to life where at times I'd thought I never had a friend in the world; at other times the crowd were all on my side, even Sam Barter the bosun from whom, in reality, I did learn so much.

Epilogue

In my preface, I wrote most seamen will remember their first ship as no other and now the story of my first trip has been told it's probably best I speak for myself.

I must admit, when I joined the *Willesden* I was like any other boy of my age, rather green to the way of life, and especially with regard to women and those who dress up as them. The reason for this naiveté was simply because schools only taught what they wanted you to know, and not what you should know.

Having been brought up in a narrow-minded era, one which many call a backward Victorian society, my first real lessons in life came when I sat in the mess room of the *Willesden* listening to the gossip of the sailors. There I heard all kinds of stories of good and bad times, of hardships and of strife, but they all seemed to end involving encounters with women. It was there in the mess room of the *Willesden* I learned the first ropes of life, and fortunately for me anyway, all those 'taboo' lessons of the birds and the bees which had been denied me at school were listened to and well heeded.

I feel – as well as being the best way to broaden the mind – joining the Merchant Navy was the greatest school of education I could ever have had. For me, my schooling in life only began when I joined the *Willesden*, although since leaving that vessel I've sailed on better ships, and worse (an awful lot worse). As well as having had the pleasure of serving with such a good bunch of men, I will always remember my first ship the *Willesden* as no other.

Sometime in 1954 and about nine months or so after I'd paid off from the *Willesden*, I was serving as a JOS on the *Sekondi* of Elder Dempster

Lines; we were five months through an eight month voyage. Laying at anchor in the Lagos river one afternoon, another ordinary seaman and I were engaged in soojying the lower mizzenmast. I was sitting in a bosun's chair doing the after fleet.

In the hot afternoon with the cargo tents rigged over the hatches for the Kroo Boys, and a few small craft going up and down the river, I heard from astern the unmistakable sound of a Burmeister Wayne diesel engine floating across the still waters. It was a sound just like a rickety old typewriter and one I knew I'd heard before. To me it could only come from one source, and as I turned around, there sure enough slowly coming up on our starboard side was the *Willesden.*

She must have been well over fifty yards away as she went past at about four knots, the deck crowd were all at stations. I looked over the ship from my vantage point where on her focs'le head was one particular person who had a slightly more rotund appearance than the rest. I knew by his shape it could only be 'my first bosun', and as he appeared to be looking towards me I gave him a wave. He waved back! This made me wonder if he knew who he was waving at; surely if he did know he might have shook his fist instead.

The next evening at about 19h00, I got a boat from our river anchorage to the *Willesden* which was now alongside just half a mile away. The *Sekondi* was a hungry ship, so as well as the fact I thought there might be some leftovers from teatime, I hoped I'd be invited for some eats. Otherwise I suppose the visit was more for curiosity than anything else. I walked up the gangway I'd been up and down so many times before, once again I had the strange feeling I'd had when I first stepped aboard over a year ago. I made my way aft then made my acquaintance with a few of the crowd who were sitting around the after bitts. It seemed so odd to see the crowd of strangers who were the deck department, it almost seemed as though they were on the wrong ship.

It wasn't long before I came face to face with my old friend the bosun, who appeared quite pleased to see me saying he appreciated my visit, Fred was alongside him.

When I first joined the *Willesden* I'd just turned sixteen, and compared to now a year or so later at seventeen, I'd grown about four inches and put on an extra two stones in weight. This feat of nature was warmly applauded by 'Sam' who, due to my extra growth in height and weight, asked me if the 'Monkey Boat' I was on was a good feeder. I told him the *Sekondi* was extremely hungry, and just as bad as another ship I'd been on after I'd left the *Willesden.* Fred, who was always amusing with his dry sense of humour, remarked it was quite obvious I'd been on some hungry ships since he last saw me, because all my pimples had gone.

The bosun didn't look quite so tall any more, and I told him it'd been relatively easy for me to identify him as the *Willesden* went past in the river. I asked him if he realized it was me who was waving to him from the mizzen mast, he replied yes, he knew it was me alright, he didn't know how, he just knew. During the conversation I told the bosun and Fred I still spent a lot of time drawing pictures of ships, the diaries I'd written had all been put away and would one day be published, and he, the bosun, was to be the star of the story. The bosun thought such a story would be amusing, and told me I mustn't forget to mention the many times when he'd turned a 'blind eye' to some of my activities. He reminded me of the drawing of the *Willesden* I owed him, and I in turn reminded him of the three winch beds on the fore deck I never did.

The conversation continued and I was questioned regarding my progress since leaving the *Willesden*. I related my adventures to the *Twickenham* Twins, telling them of my rude awakening on other ships I'd since served in. The bosun and Fred listened and laughed as I told them after having left the *Willesden*, I'd signed on the *Baron Inverclyde*. How the ship had been bought on the stocks from a Swedish company, who'd refused her on the acceptance trials as the ship was too slow. The *Baron Inverclyde* had been launched from the very same John Redhead's yard where I'd joined the *Willesden* in May 1953 and no doubt was one of the ships I'd seen in the process of being built.

The 'Baron Boat' had experienced great difficulty in getting a crowd, and at first I couldn't think why such a lovely clean ship on her maiden voyage, with single berth accommodation was so unwanted. I was soon to find out. While the ship had been in South Shields early in January 1954, efforts were being made to round up a deck crowd; there was only myself, another ordinary seamen and the bosun for the first couple of days. One job I took part in, during the first two days, was to haul aboard some tatty second-hand berthing ropes which had been acquired from Redhead's for the ship's use; then repairing them with the appropriate eye or short splices. The 'Baron Boat' eventually signed a crowd, then left South Shields a few days later than the company would have liked. The voyage was to the West Indies for a sugar cargo. When we left South Shields one day in January 1954, the eight to twelve watch didn't take part in letting go to save paying them overtime.

I'd signed on as a JOS for the voyage, however because there was no deck boy I was made peggy; at first I didn't want the job but it soon turned out to be much better than I'd thought. I didn't have half as much to do as I did on the *Willesden*, and the bosun had told me to book an hour's overtime each day. After we'd cleared the English Channel the bosun asked me to sign for my overtime, which he took to Mr. Campbell the first mate. Later on in the day, I was sitting on number five hatch when I saw Mr. Campbell advancing at speed down the deck. He was coming in my direction waving a piece of paper which was the overtime sheet. He looked as though he was in a state of severe shock and wanted to know where I'd worked all the overtime. After a while the huge error of my being awarded an hour a day was highlighted to the peggy's job, and Mr. Campbell most reluctantly agreed to it being approved. At the time I had fourteen hours overtime at 1/6 an hour amounting to 21/- but worse was to follow. An hour or so later, Mr. Campbell approached me, and told me after a discussion with Captain Gordon-Robb, it had been decided to dispense with the peggy job, and everyone should do their own washing-up, the watch on deck would do the scrubbing out of the accommodation.

Sam Barter the bosun and Fred, who listened with undisguised glee to my tale of woe, then poured out more beer for themselves. I wasn't offered a drink nor an invitation to eat so I continued with my lamentable tale. I told of the food on the 'Baron Boat' which was absolutely the bare minimum; the gash bucket was always empty because everybody ate all their food and even sucked on the bones – there didn't appear to be any seagulls following the ship either. The first Saturday out was full of drama, all hands had to turn to at 09h00 washing down for an hour, I was soon to discover this was the 'blood hour' in which the hands can be turned to washing down the decks without extra pay. While the washing-down was in progress, Captain Gordon-Robb stood watching, hands on hips, and appeared to be gloating. I only ever spoke to the captain a couple of times during the voyage, but he wasn't one I enjoyed conversing with; he was rather softly spoken having a cold cynical tone; it was quite clear to all in the crowd the mates were terrified of him. On the first Sunday out we had a chicken dinner and I was not the only one to have a chicken wing on my plate. We soon found out most of the legs and breasts had gone into the saloon. The ship arrived at its berth in San Pedro de Macoris after about two weeks where the loading was quickly completed. Then on sailing day came the biggest shock of them all – Captain Gordon-Robb ordered the deck and engine department out on the deck by number five hatch where he made an announcement. He said he hoped we'd all enjoyed the outward passage, the frequent showers, and plenty of fresh water to do our dhobying, because on the homeward run to

London things were about to change. He said the fresh water tanks were being pumped out so an extra 100 tons of cargo could be carried. We would be issued with one bucket of water per day per man – more than the Board of Trade scale – and the allowance would have to suffice for our cooking, drinking, washing, and bathing. The trip back to the UK was only marked by the fact everyone who lived aft had B.O. and nobody had washed their clothes. We had water to drink but by the time the ship arrived in the English Channel there was no water left in the ship; even the steam cylinders of the winches had been drained. There were three of the sailors who never even had one single penny of overtime for the entire voyage. Mr. Campbell had sent for them asking they sign a blank sheet; they refused and gave mate some verbal abuse, the captain overheard, and all three were told they would be getting a DR in their books for conduct. Eventually the ship arrived at the sugar berth in London. Some of the more senior hands in the crowd summoned the Board of Trade officials as well as the National Union of Seamen and there was uproar. On complaining to the National Union of Seamen representative, the three men were offered further employment on the ship to cover up the bad discharge they were about to receive. It was claimed the purpose of this offer of future employment was simply to avoid the company having to pay the rail fares of the three men. Earlier on, the bosun and then Mr. Campbell had approached me offering further employment for the next voyage, I refused, and the bosun told me he himself was getting out after just the one trip. I never found out if the three men did receive a bad discharge in their books because I left the ship as quickly as I could; but one thing I was sure of, was with my 21/- I had the most overtime in the deck, engine, and stewards' department.

With a big smile on his face, Sam Barter rubbed his hands and told me at one time, and not even so long ago, just about all deep sea ships were the same. He then asked me about the *Sekondi* on which I was presently serving.

Once again I gave an unfavourable report, stating my present ship was just as bad as the Baron Boat in some ways and probably the only advantage was we had water to drink. However, the cooking by the Nigerian galley staff was disgraceful and the food completely inadequate. The ship had been out for five months and at present the deck department had opted to go on their Board of Trade scale. The *Sekondi* was presently loading for the USA where we'd already done one trip and we hoped this would be the last. Shortly after, the chief steward was sacked in Lagos and replaced. The Board of Trade scale then ended.

So ended my visit to the *Willesden*, and judging by his facial expressions I think its bosun Sam Barter was more than a little pleased I'd had a bit of a hard time since leaving him. It was as though he was thinking, 'You could have still been on the *Willesden* if you'd behaved a bit better.'

I said my goodbyes to the bosun and Fred. The *Willesden* was only in for a short stay and her discharging was almost complete. The next morning when I turned to I looked over to where the *Willesden* had been laying, she'd gone, and I never saw the ship again.

§

It wasn't until I left my last ship in 1990 when I went through the diaries I'd written in 1953; it was then I decided to make a start on my 'record of the times'. I sent away for and received from The Newfoundland Memorial, a copy of the articles of agreement of the two voyages of the MV *Willesden* in 1953. Upon receiving the photostat copy, I found it so strange to once again see the names of the two crews who had been my first shipmates. Stranger still was the fact, in my mind's eye I could still visualise every one of their faces, even the engineers. It was amusing to see in the records the size of the pay-offs of some of the crowd and especially the chippy. The bosun had always claimed he was so tight-fisted he'd be the richest man in the graveyard when he died. In truth the chippy never drank or smoked, never had a sub or went ashore, and as far as I know never spent anything in the chief steward's bond. The bosun's assessment of Achmid the chippy was certainly a correct one, because according to the records I now possess, Achmid had the biggest pay-off in the ship except for the captain.

In 1999 and from my diaries, I began writing the manuscript *A Deck Boy's Diary* the object of which was simply to make, or to keep, a record of what life was like on board one ship of the Merchant Navy before the service disappeared into oblivion. Although I'd kept a fairly accurate diary of events, I thought it would be nice to see if I could make contact with somebody who had been on the ship with me – to verify the manuscript before it went to press.

Bearing in mind many of the crew of the *Willesden* would no longer be with us, for at the time of writing even I am sixty-two, I now had all the addresses of my former shipmates, or at least the addresses they had forty-six years ago. I took a long shot and spent quite some time going through telephone directories to see if I could find if there was anybody still around. I was just about to give up when with the very last attempt I made contact with Fred Hodges my cabin mate.

Fred is now seventy-six and he shouldn't really have been a problem to find in the first place. He told me as I spoke to him on the phone, not only was he still at the same Somerset address, he'd been born in the house, as had his father and grandfather. I went to see him, and except for the white beard he now owned, it was the same old Fred.

I gave him a copy of the first draft of the manuscript I'd written, and we talked about our former ship. Fred and his long time buddy the bosun had stayed on the *Willesden* to the end, but the sad news he gave me was Captain Grist had been murdered on board the *Willesden* in 1957. The captain had been shot after an argument with the ship's agent at a Phillipine anchorage, and despite all efforts – taking him in a lifeboat some thirty miles to the nearest hospital – the captain died in the boat. The chief steward Mr. Perkins had retired with all his hard-earned money to Canada. Sam Barter the bosun, who was Fred's lifelong friend had never married and had died some years back in 1989. Fred had also managed to remain single and after forty-five years of sea service, first throughout the war in the Royal Navy, Fred had made his last trip to sea in 1984.

During our conversation, Fred confessed it was himself and the bosun who had aided and abetted in the misappropriation of cargo, namely six sacks of spuds, while the ship was in the Red Sea. This finally put an end to the mystery of who pulled up the spuds and battened down the hatch.

Another amazing event which occurred on the *Willesden* and which has only just been brought to light, was the signing on at Tilbury of my AB cabin mate R. Walker. At the time of his engagement, it was the London dockers who told me Old Stan had once served aboard the *Cutty Sark* on her last voyage under the red ensign. At the time I hardly knew of the *Cutty Sark* or what it represented except it was an old sailing ship; also, it had cost me a shilling and a sixteen mile walk from Blyth to Newcastle in 1953. I'd forgotten all about the incident of Old Stan until the present year of 1999, when I carried out some investigations into the man.

After carrying out some research into the crews of the *Cutty Sark*, I found in his publication *Crews Of the Cutty Sark* written by S F Bailey and published by The Cutty Sark Society, there had been in fact a 23 year old AB from Kirkcaldy named R Walker who signed on the ship on May 2 1889. He later paid off as second mate on January 17 1890. This was the last voyage of the *Cutty Sark* under the red ensign. This may or may not be the same Scotsman who shared my cabin, but if as I believe it possibly was, then Old Stan my cabin mate was eighty-seven years old at the time of joining the *Willesden*.

In 1991, I was supplied by the National Maritime Museum with a record of the career years of the MV *Willesden*. It would seem after the murder of Captain Grist in his cabin, the vessel was sold on returning to the UK after serving the company for twelve years.

It would appear the last owners of the former *Willesden*, The Leo Shipping Company were some kind of merchants who specialised in scrapping ships, because after they'd purchased the vessel in 1966 she was renamed *Golden Wind* , then in December of the same year, she was sent to a scrap yard at Hiroshima.

Name of Ship	Date	Owners
1 *Empire Canning*	1944 Launched – Dundee	Ministry of War Transport
2 *Willesden*	1946	Britain SS Co. – Watts Watts & Co.
3 *Golden Lambda*	1958	World Wide Shipping Co.
4 *Marine Explorer*	1960	Neptune Shipping Co.
5 *East Vin*	1962	Viking Shipping Co.
6 *Wasa Bay*	1963	Marine Navigation Co.
7 *Golden Wind*	1966 Scrapped - Hiroshima	Leo Shipping Co.

Glossary

A

AB	An abbreviation for Able Bodied. One who is certificated as a first class seaman.
Abeam	At a ninety degree angle to the fore and aft line.
Aft	To the rear of – Behind – Astern of – Abaft.
Aloft	Above – Higher up – Up the mast.

B

Ballast –	The extra weight (usually seawater) that is loaded onto a ship after it has discharged its cargo. This is to lessen the risk of the ship capsising. See – Light Ship – In Ballast.
Backspring	A berthing rope that's usually made of wire. It is secured to the bitts and led forward to the quayside to prevent the ship moving aft. See Head Spring.
Beam	One of the heavy steel girders that traverse the hatch of the cargo hold.
Beam	The maximum width measurement of the ship.
Beam Ends	A ship is said to be on its beam ends when it is laying on its side.
Beam Sea	When the sea approaches the ship side on.
Binnacle	The casing which houses the magnetic compass.
Bitts	The steel bollard posts on which a ship's berthing ropes are secured.
Bollard	A fixture that allows ropes to pass around or be secured to.
Boot Topping	The expanse of ship's side from the water line down.
Bosun	Shortened version of Boatswain – The senior deck hand.
Bow	Bows – The forepart of the hull – The overhang of the focs'le head.
Block	A sheaved pulley through which a rope may be led.
Blue Peter	Letter P of the international code of signals which signifies that a ship is shortly due to sail.
Bulkhead	A dividing steel wall between the ship's cargo holds. Walls on ships are generally referred to as bulkheads.
Bulwark	A raised steel wall on the ship's side which performs the same as guard rails.

C

Carried Away	Broken – Snapped – Parted.
Ceiling	The wooden centre square at the bottom of a ship's hold.
Coaming	A raised parapet found at each door opening to stop water coming through that doorway. A hatch coaming is a raised parapet about thirty inches in height to stop water entering the hold.
Companionway	The stairway leading to the accommodation.
Chippy	The ship's carpenter.
Channels	A derogatory name given to a person who is unable to sleep or eat and is over anxious for the ship to pay off.
Chain Stopper	A length of chain used for temporarily holding the weight of a wire rope until it is made fast onto the bitts or cleats.

Coir	See Runner. A length of matting used in the accommodation.
Collier	A coal-carrying ship.
Crowd	The personnel of the deck department – The sailors.
Company's Man	Any person who has signed a company contract. Also a derogatory name given to a parsimonious person who constantly saves stores for the company in order to gain the favourable attention of his superiors.

D

Deep Sea	Foreign Going.
Deadweight Tons	See Tons and Tonnage.
Deck Head	The 'ceiling' of a compartment. The underside of the roof above.
Deck Quoite	A single strand of rope that is laid back into itself to form a circle, it is finished off with an overhand knot with the ends being tucked.
Dhobying	The washing of clothing
Dodger	A width of canvas used on bridge wings or guard-rails to curtail the wind.
Down By the Head	When a ship is improperly balanced and is overloaded forward. Also a slang term used to describe a person who has an abundance of some particular item.
Draught Marks	The Roman numeral figures on the stem and stern post of a ship that indicate the amount of water from that point to the keel.
Dunnage	Miscellaneous planks of wood normally used with the stowing of cargo.

E

EDH	Efficient Deck Hand. A certificated seaman
Even Keel	When a ship is evenly balanced and neither rolling nor pitching.
Eyes	The eyes of ship – That part of the focs'le head that's the most forward – over the stem.

F

Fathom	Nautical measurement that equals six feet – Two yards – One thousand eight hundred and twenty-nine millimeters.
Fairlead	A lead for the ship's berthing or tow ropes. A roller fairlead does a similar job.
Farmer	The seaman who has no wheel to do during a watch.
Fid	A wooden implement used in the splicing of fibre rope.
Fidley	The skylight to the engine room.
Fire Bars	Protective steel bars that fit across the galley range to prevent cooking utensils from rolling off in heavy weather.
Flaked Out	When rope is laid out on the deck. Also, a term to describe someone who has collapsed through exhaustion or drink.
Focs'le	Abbreviation of Forecastle. Also a name given to the sailors' accommodation, whatever part of the ship it may be in.
Foredeck	That part of the maindeck which is forward of amidships.
Forrard	Forward.
Force Twelve	Wind speed of sixty-four knots or over – Approximately 75 mph.

G

Gantline	A two inch general purpose fibre rope.
Gear	Any moveable item on a ship. Also a name given to clothing
Galley	A ship's kitchen
Galley Wireless	The grapevine of a ship. A source of unfounded rumours
Geordie	A native of Tyneside.
Greaser	An engine room rating of a motor vessel
Green'un	A large wave.
Gross Tons	See Tons and Tonnage.

H

Halyard	A small diameter rope used in the hauling up of signal flags to the masthead or yardarm. Originally from the words 'Haul Yard' a sailing ship term.
Handy Billy	A small tackle of two inches or less that consists of a double and single block. When rove to disadvantage the velocity ratio is three and when rove to advantage it is four.
Hard Tack	Emergency lifeboat rations of biscuits. Biscuits that are most nourishing but rock hard and are often soaked before being eaten.
Hatchboard	A section of timber about five x two feet that fits between the beams that traverse the cargo hatch.
Headspring	A berthing rope usually a wire rope. It is secured to the bitts and led aft to prevent the ship moving ahead. See Backspring
Heaving Line	Small diameter rope that is designed for use when a ship is berthing alongside.
Hinney	A term of endearment used by Tynesiders that probably means Honey.
Hog. Hogging	In heavy weather, the stress caused on a vessel's hull when the 'midship section is lifted by one wave leaving both ends without suspension thereby causing stress at the centre of the keel. Hogging can also be caused when a ship is aground.
Holidays	Sundays at sea – Slang terms generally used in painting, where the painter has left gaps in his work.
Holystone	Blocks of sandstone or similar, that are normally attached to pole handles. They are used to barbarise or scrub the wooden decks in conjunction with the washing-down. Holystoning is referred to by sailors as 'Bible Practice'.
House Flag	A flag flown from the masthead that will identify the ship's owner.

I

In Ballast	A vessel without cargo that has loaded some weight to help prevent it capsising, this is usually sea water in a specially designed tank and normally amidships.

J

JOS	Junior Ordinary Seaman.

K

Kit or Kid	Food containers such as pots, pans and trays.
Knight heads	Originally named after the chocks that supported a sailing vessel's bowsprit. In modern times, it is the name given to the small sheltering at the most forward end of the focs'le head.
Knots	A nautical measurement of speed combined with distance. Each Knot of speed is equivalent to 6,080 feet travelled in one hour (a statute land mile is 5,760 feet).
Kroo Boys	These are members of the Kroo tribe from Sierra Leone. They embark at Freetown for working cargo around the West African coast.

L

Lazarette	A small hatch space uncertified for the carrying of cargo, used mainly for the stowage of the berthing ropes and deck stores.
Lee Side	That side of the ship which is away from the wind and weather.
Lifelines	Ropes stretched across or along the deck for handholds in heavy weather.
Line	Rope of less than two inches circumference.
Liner	A ship that is on a regular run.
Light Ship	When a ship's cargo has been discharged and the holds are empty. This may have the same meaning as a ship in ballast.
Lizard	A short length of rope with a thimble spliced into one end. See Pennant.

M

Maindeck	The longest unbroken deck of a ship, and usually the upperdeck.
Making Way	A term used to describe a ship moving through the water.
Manila	A superior natural fibre rope, its fibres originating from Manila in the Phillipines.
Marlin Spike	A tool used in the splicing of wire ropes.
Monkey Island	The open deck that is above the wheelhouse.
Monkey Boat	A ship belonging to Elder Dempster Lines.

N

Norwegian Steam	By hand – Without the use of auxiliary power – Muscle power. – Brute strength.
Nett Tons	See Tons and Tonnage.

O

One Bell	Fifteen minutes before the next watch comes on duty.
Old Man	The Captain.
Old Man	A statuary fairlead lead set at an angle for a berthing rope.
On Her Marks	When a ship has loaded down to the Load or Plimsoll Line.

P

Passage	The Sailing between two seaports.
Passage	When something is thrown overboard, it is referred to as having been 'Given a Passage'.
Pegged Out	A cribbage term, also a version that has been adapted to describe a person deceased.
Pennant	A signal flag.
Pennant	A short length of rope with a thimble spliced into each end. See Lizard.
Poop-Deck	Poop-housing – The poop deck is in general a raised deck on the after end of a vessel. The poop housing is a structure on that deck.
Pooped	When a following sea that travels faster than the ship, sweeps over its stern engulfing it.

R

Range	Ranged – Ranging – When a ship moves up and down the quayside in a fore and aft motion.
Rope Stopper	A length of rope used for the purpose of holding the weight on a larger rope while that larger rope is being secured.
Rove	Reeve – When a rope is led through a sheaved block.
Ring Bolt	A steel ring that is mostly fastened to the deck on an eye plate.
Runner	Coir – A length of matting used in the accommodation.
Runner	Wire – The wire rope that is generally used on the winches for cargo handling.

S

Saloon	The dining room for the ship's officers.
Sag	Sagging – In heavy weather the stress caused on a ship's hull, when both ends of the ship are lifted simultaneously causing strain on the midship section. Can also be caused when a ship is improperly loaded or when it is aground. See Hog.
Schooner Rigged.	As well as being the fore and aft rig of a sailing vessel, it is a slang name given to any seaman who is short of clothing.
Scouser	A native of Liverpool.
Scuppers	The waterways on deck or the waste drains.
Scuttle	The purposeful sinking of a ship. Also a name often for a porthole.
Serving	Tarred hemp that is wound around a wire rope to give added protection.
Seven Bells	Forty minutes before the next watch comes on duty.
Sheave	The wheel at the centre of a block.
Shoulder	The forward part of the hull where it broadens out from the flare of the bows.
Shipped	When something comes aboard a vessel.
Shrouds	The wire ropes that support or stay the masts.
Shifting Boards	Heavy planks of wood, used in the construction of a dividing wall to prevent the cargo shifting.

Skinned Out	This term has the same meaning as 'Backed Out' and refers to a person who has deserted his ship.
Sky Pilot	A vicar or other church dignitary.
Smoko	Tea or coffee break.
Soojying	The washing of paint work.
SOS	Senior Ordinary Seaman.
Sounding Pipe	A pipe projection coming out of the main deck permitting the insertion of a chalked rod and line which will give an indication of water or oil level in a particular tank, bilge or other compartment.
Stem	The most forward part of a ship's hull.
Stern	The after end of a ship.

T

Table	The platform on a mast mainly used to support lead blocks for the derricks.
Taffrail	The guardrail at the aftermost part of the ship.
Tarred Hemp	Rope or line made of hemp and treated with Stockholm Tar.
Tons and Tonnage	A ship's tonnage is calculated in different manners. The gross tonnage of a ship is measured on cubic capacity, ie each one hundred cubic feet equals one ton. The nett tonnage is the gross tonnage minus all the space taken up by the accommodation, engine room and store rooms. The displacement tonnage is measured by the amount of water a ship will displace and usually refers to warships. The deadweight tonnage is the amount of cargo a ship can carry.
Tramp	A ship which has no regular run and is available for hire.
Truck	The round plate-like object at the very top of the mast, it usually has one or two sheaves in it to allow for a signal halyard.
Turn To	When a person begins working.
'Tween Deck	An abbreviation for a deck that is 'between' the upper or main deck, and the lower hold. A ship may have more than one 'tween deck.
Two Black Balls	A hoisted signal which signifies the ship displaying them has broken down, is not under command, and unable to manoeuvre.
Two Blocks	Chock-a-Block – Chocker – When a tackle is rove hard up.

W

Watch	A period of four hours duty. There are six watches in each day – Middle – Morning – Forenoon – Afternoon – Evening – and Night Watch. On some ships and especially warships, the Evening Watch is split into two parts and known as the First and Second Dog Watches.
Warped	When a ship is hauled up the quayside by hand, or windlass power.
Weighed Anchor	As an anchor is being hauled in, the point when the anchor is clear of the seabed is known as Weighed Anchor or Anchors Aweigh.
Woodbine Funnel	A tall thin funnel usually associated with coal-burning vessels.
Weather Side	That side of the ship which the weather or wind is coming from.

Annex to the glossary

Although at all times it's been the author's objective to keep the manuscript as close as possible to its original form of 1953, there has been one change which should be explained in order for the manuscript not to be altered. This is the description of the coinage of the realm which was in use in 1953 and this is mentioned in the manuscript a number of times. The purpose of making this explanation is not totally for the readers of today! They may well understand the value of 'Five Bob' or 'Six and a tanner,' but it is for the readers of tomorrow, who may be scratching their heads wondering what two shillings, a florin, two bob, or 2/- was.

In the year of 1953, Great Britain used an extremely antiquated and rather complicated monetary system.

A £1 had the same meaning in 1953 as it has today in 1999, but the £1 of 1953 had an entirely different structure. It was made up of twenty units called shillings, and each of these shillings was made up of twelve pence. Therefore, there was two hundred and forty pennies to each pound.

The slang name for a shilling was 'A Bob' – Five shillings was 'Five Bob' – and so on for each of the twenty shillings of the £1.

A shilling was written as 1/- and Five Shillings as 5/-.

In the writing of a monetary figure, any number of the twelve pennies in a shilling could be added to a shilling with the use of a slash, for example, 'The rate of overtime was 1/6 an hour,' this meant one shilling and six pence an hour. A carton of cigarettes cost 7/6 meaning seven shillings and six pence.

A 'Tanner' was the slang word used for sixpence. Therefore, when speaking of money, 'Six and a Tanner' in value and in slang terms, was six shillings and sixpence.

In 1971 the old monetary system changed to what it is in 1999.

Quite simply there were now, one hundred 'New Pence' to the pound; and gone were the crowns, half crowns, florins, shillings, bobs and tanners.

Although it kept its name, the value of the penny changed too. There were now just 100 pence to take the place of the 240 in 1953.

Index

Acknowledgements and Sources of Information

In the making of this publication there are a number of people who have contributed greatly to its being. As well as the men of the Merchant Navy from whom I learned so much, there are others who have helped with their profound advice. The people who at their own expense, have supplied me with information and photographs as well as those who have given so much of their time in helping in the preparation of this manuscript.

First and foremost I would like to mention Fred Hodges who was my cabin mate on board the *Willesden* in 1953. Fred has gone some way in supplying valuable information and a number of photographs, as well as reading through and verifying the manuscript. The remainder of the people to whom I'm indebted follow in alphabetical order.

Captain Graeme Cubbins of T&J Harrison Lines for his advice and help in securing information and photographs. Captain Cubbins is presently the keeper of the T&J Harrison Museum, Covent Gardens, Liverpool.

Charlie Hobson of The Liverpool Retired Seamen and former bosun of the Liverpool pilot vessel *Edmund Gardiner* for his valuable contribution of information and photographs.

Janes Fighting Ships 1952 – 1953.

Jimmy Maguire of Carrington, Newcastle NSW for his photographic contribution.

The National Maritime Museum for supplying information on the MV *Willesden.*

Newfoundland seamen's archives for supplying the official logs of the MV *Willesden.*

Canadian Pacific Afloat by George Musk.

Sail Training and Cadet Ships by A. Underhill – Brown Son & Ferguson.

Tommy O'Leary of the Liverpool Retired Seamens' Institute, the former bosun of the *City Of Durban* for supplying information and photographs.

A Potted Histories of ships

In this section are some of the ships which are mentioned in the main manuscript.

Adviser
Built by Lithgow at Port Glasgow in 1939 at a cost of £193,676 – sister ship to the *Barrister.* Dimensions; – GRT.6348 – Dwt. 9000. Length OAL.459.25 ft. – Beam – 56.5 – Draught – 32.17. Engines – Triple Expansion, coal – 14.5 knots. Maiden voyage to South Africa April 1939, Capt. JT Ling. Damaged by *Clan MacFarlane* whilst berthed in Liverpool Aug 1939. Attacked in convoy by German heavy cruiser *Admiral Hipper* on 25 December 1940. Took part in the second phase of the Madagascar campaign in 1942, then in the same year 15 November she was torpedoed in the Indian Ocean but managed to reach Durban for repairs. October 1943, converted to arry 56 passengers. Laid up at Blyth Apr – Sept. 1952 and converted to burn oil. Main engines broke down whilst entering Cape Town in January 1955 where the ship suffered damage on colliding with the quay wall. Sold for £64,000 and arrived at Tamaise for breaking up 4 Sept. 1960.

Baron Inverclyde
Built by John Readheads of South Shields, this vessel was owned by H. Hogarth of Ardrossan. 6000 tons – Maiden voyage January 1954 – Capt. L. Gordon Robb.

Bradford City
Launched November 1942, completed February 1943 by Doxfords Sunderland for the Leeds Shipping Co. that was owned by Sir William Reardon Smith. GRT 7266, Dimensions; 428.8 x 56.5 ft. Sold to Vergocean S.S. Co. of London in 1962 and re-named *Vercharmain.* Sold on to the Jebshun Shipping Co. in 1968 and renamed *Shun Wah.* Arrived at Todatsu Japan in May 1972 for breaking up.

Brittanic
A sister ship to the *Georgic*, but they differed slightly in external appearance. With a speed of 18 knots, these vessels were the largest motor ships on the North Atlantic passenger service. The *Brittanic* originally carried 479 Cabin, 557 Tourist, and 506 third class passengers. The White Star Line used the pair on the Liverpool, Cobh, New York route but on amalgamation of the Cunard and the White Star Lines, the Cunard altered the route to London, Havre, Southampton, New York in April 1935. Requisitioned by the government for use as a trooper in September 1939. Reconditioned as a passenger vessel and resumed service in May 1948 until she ended her last voyage on December 2 1960.

Calliope HMS

City of Liverpool
Belonging to Ellerman Bucknalls, the ship was built in 1948.

Clan McNair
Built for the Clan Line in 1923, the vessel was scrapped in 1952 at Blyth.

Consuelo
This steamship belonging to Ellerman Wilsons of Hull was built in 1937.

Empress of Australia
Originally named *De Grasse* this vessel was ordered in 1918 as the *Suffren* and laid down on 3 March 1920, but her launching by Cammel Lairds of Birkenhead didn't take place until 23 February 1924. First owners were the Compagnie Generale Transatlantique (French Line). Of 17,707 GRT Her dimensions were 552 x 72 x 30 with a speed of 16 knots. – Seized by the Germans in 1940 she was used as an accommodation ship in the River Gironde near Bordeaux. On 30 Aug 1944 she was scuttled but refloated by Chantiers et Ateliers de Saint-Nazaire-Penhoet and a single one replaced the two original funnels. – Tonnage increased to 18,435 Gross. – Returned to service on the Havre to New York route in July 1947. – As a makeshift replacement for the burned *Empress of Canada*, she was bought by CPR on 26 March 1953 and renamed *Empress of Australia* on 27 April 1953. Sailed the following day for Quebec. On 5 December 1955 sailed from Quebec on her last transatlantic voyage for the CPR. – On 9 January 1956 the ship left Liverpool for Gareloch for laying up. – 15 February 1956 sold to Fratelli Grimaldi of Genoa and renamed *Venezuela*. – 16 March 1962 ran aground off Cannes then laid up at Genoa. 28 August 1962 sold for scrap and broken up at Spezia.

Empress of France
Launched at John Browns on 24 January 1928 as the *Duchess of Bedford* this vessel was 20,123 GRT. Other dimensions being 582 x 75 x 32 She was one of four sisters the other three being, *Duchess of Atholl, Duchess of Richmond*, and *Duchess of York*. Requisitioned for service as a trooper on 28 September 1939. Heavily shelled being one of the last British ships to escape from Singapore on that seaports fall to the Japanese. On 3 March 1947 arrived at Fairfields for refitting and renamed *Empress of France*. 1 September 1948 resumed service a passenger vessel. 20 December 1960 arrived at Newport Mon for breaking up. The Empress bar was bought and incorporated as the Empress Room in the Barry Hotel Newport Mon. in May 1961. The ship's bell was presented to, Div. Movements, Army HQ Ottawa.

Empress of Scotland
Originally named *Empress of Japan* on her launch date of December 17, 1929. GRT 26,032 Dimensions 640 x 84. X 32. – Maiden voyage began on 14 June 1930 with a record breaking crossing from Liverpool to Quebec of 5days 5 hours; her best Atlantic crossing was from Rimouski of Quebec to Cumbrae in Scotland in 4days 14 hours and 42 minutes. – In the Pacific in May 1935 she created another record of six days eight hours 39 minutes between Yokohama and Honolulu with an average speed of 22.16 knots, then from Hawaai to Victoria at 22.37 knots. – Requisitioned for wartime service as a troop-ship at the outbreak of WW2. Renamed *Empress of Scotland* on 16 October 1942 then released from trooping duties on 3 May 1948. Steamed over 600,000 miles as a trooper. Refitted for Liverpool to Quebec service, to run a 21-day round trip. – GRT increased to 26,313. Commenced her post war services on May 9, 1950. – In April 1952 her masts were shortened to allow passage under the Quebec Bridge to Montreal. The ships first visit to Montreal began from Liverpool on 13 May 1952. – On 25 November 1957 the

vessel was laid up at Liverpool and sold to the Hamburg-Atlantic Line. – January 1, 1958 left Liverpool for Belfast as the last ever three-funnelled passenger vessel to use the port. 22 January 1958 arrived at Howaldt shipyard Hamburg and renamed *Hanseatic,* tonnage increased to 30,030 GRT and the dummy after funnel being removed. – 21 July1958 sailed from Cuxhaven for New York via Southampton and Cobh. On 7 September 1966 caught fire at New York then on 29 September 1966 towed to Hamburg by the tugs *Atlantic* and *Pacific,* where she was found to be beyond economical repair and broken up.

Georgic
Built by Harland & Wolff at Belfast for the White Star Line she joined her sister Brittanic as the only British motorships on the North Atlantic passenger service. She had passenger accommodation for 479 cabin class, 557 tourist, and 506 third class. Speed 18 knots Dimensions 680 x 82 x 33. Requisitioned by the Ministry of War Transport in March 1940 for trooping. As a result of an air attack the ship was heavily damaged at Port Tewfik but eventually salved from a semi submerged position. Towed to Belfast where reconstruction took place with a single funnel replacing the former two.

Gambia HMS
Developed from the *Newcastle* Class – Light Cruiser
Laid down at Swan Hunters on the Tyne on 24 July 1939 – launched 30 November 1940 and completed 21 February 1942.
Displacement tons 8,000 – Dimensions 555 x 62 x 21ft.
Armament – Nine 6inch – Eight 4inch – Sixteen 40mm – twelve 20mm – Twenty-four 2 Pounders – Six 21 inch torpedoes.
Engines – Parsons geared turbines – speed 31 knots – Complement 730 peacetime 980 wartime.

Malakand
This ship was built with her two sisters *Manaar* and *Matheran* under special licence for T&J Brocklebank and completed in December 1942. She was a replacement name for the ammunition ship which blew up whilst in Liverpool during the May Blitz of 1941. Built by Wm. Hamilton of Port Glasgow, her GRT was 8078 and dimensions 494. 7 oa x 62.7. Powered by three steam turbines, speed 15 knots; arrived at Kaohsiung in December 1966 for breaking up.

Pamir
This four masted barque was built in 1905 by Blohm& Voss of Hamburg for F. Laeisz of the same port. Registered at 3020 tons her deadweight was some 5,000 tons. She had a length of 316ft. BP. a beam of 46ft. And a depth of hold of 26ft. At the end of WW1 she was handed over to Italy as a war reparation but was bought back by F. Laeizs in 1925; then after some years in the Chilean nitrate trade was sold in 1932 to Gustaf Erikson of Finland for £4,000. Seized as a prize of war whilst in New Zealand in 1941 and after a big overhaul, she begun sailing under the NZ flag in 1943. Sold as scrap to Belgian breakers in 1951 but re-purchased with her sister *Passat* by Herr Heinz Schliewen. Both vessels were converted into auxiliary sail training ships with a 7 knot engine; also fitted was radar, echo sounding gear and wireless. She was equipped to carry between 60 and 80

cadets but because of high operating costs the Pamir was laid up at Hamburg from 1952-54. Sold by public auction she resumed sail training. The *Pamir* was lost with all but six of her crew in a North Atlantic hurricane in 1957.

Passat
Launched in 1911 by Blotim & Voss for the flying 'P' Line. Very similar in build to the *Pamir* with a Liverpool house and rigged as a four masted barque. 3,091 GRT. Used mainly in the nitrate trade she was converted to carry cadets in 1927. Now a museum ship in Sweden.

Norton
Built for R. Chapman & Son of Newcastle and at 7,195 GRT was completed August 1941. Sold to Cia. De Vapores Realma SA of Panama in 1956 she was renamed *Mastro Stelios* until she was sold on to the Chinese Government and renamed *Hoping Ssu Shi Chi,* in 1960. Transferred to China Ocean Shipping Co. in 1974 she was renamed *Ho Ping 47,* then in 1979 was again transferred and renamed *Zhan Dou 47.*

Novelist
Built to the design of T&J Harrisons of Liverpool, and completed by Harland & Wolff of Glasgow on 8 September 1940. Dimensions 423.4 x 54.5 ft. – GRT 6,133 – Engines triple expansion 3xcyl. – 11 knots.
11-12 March 1941 damaged by bombs whilst at Manchester. 11 January 1943 damaged by bombs in Bone harbour. Re-named *Phoenix* in 1961 and sent to the breakers.

San Velino
Launched in November 1943 and completed in June the following year, this 8210 GRT tanker was built for the Eagle Oil Tanker Co. of London. Dimensions; 465.3 x 59.3 Steam reciprocating engines gave her a speed of ten knots. Arrived at Grimstad in April 1962 for breaking up.

Sekondi
Built at Haverton Hill in 1948 for Elder Dempster Lines of Liverpool. – 4,811 gross tons – the ship sank in a hurricane in the Indian Ocean in 1967 whilst under East African ownership.

The Lady Charrington

Twickenham
Built for the Britain Steamship Co. (Watts Watts) this vessel of 4826 GRT was launched on 17 September 1940 and completed in November of the same year. She was a sister to the *Tottenham* that was captured and sunk by the *Atlantis.* Dimensions; 417.6 x 56ft. Engines 3xcyl. steam reciprocating 11 knots. On 15 July 1943 on passage from Hull to Buenos Aires she was torpedoed by U. 135 whilst in convoy OS 51 off the Canary Islands. She suffered damage to the forefoot but remained afloat. After an initial tow, arrived at Dakar under her own steam on 31 July. Makeshift repairs were carried out then she sailed for UK on 21 October 1944 arriving at Middle Docks South Shields on 15 December 1944

for repairs. After serving Watts Watts & Co. she was sold to the Great Eastern Shipping Co. of Bombay in 1958 and renamed *Jag Mata* then in 1963 was scrapped at Bombay.

Tudor Queen.
Built for the British Channel Island Shipping Co. Ltd. and completed February 1941. Sold to British Channel Traders in 1946. Sold on again to the Queenship Navigation Ltd. .in 1947 and used extensively on the north east coast as a collier. Purchased by Coast Lines in 1959 then in the same year sent to Troon for breaking up.

CLASSIC
MARINE PUBLICATIONS

Reader's Notes

Reader's Notes

Reader's Notes